108 QUESTIONS & ANSWERS ON MUTUAL FUNDS & SIP

108 QUESTIONS & ANSWERS ON MUTUAL FUNDS & SIP

Third Edition

PARIMAL ADE & GAURAV JAIN
Founders, InvestYadnya.in

INDIA • SINGAPORE • MALAYSIA

Copyright © Yadnya Investments 2023
All Rights Reserved.

Hardcase ISBN: 979-8-89475-514-4
Paperback ISBN: 978-1-94758-632-1

This book has been published with all efforts taken to make the material error-free after the consent of the author. However, the author and the publisher do not assume and hereby disclaim any liability to any party for any loss, damage, or disruption caused by errors or omissions, whether such errors or omissions result from negligence, accident, or any other cause.

While every effort has been made to avoid any mistake or omission, this publication is being sold on the condition and understanding that neither the author nor the publishers or printers would be liable in any manner to any person by reason of any mistake or omission in this publication or for any action taken or omitted to be taken or advice rendered or accepted on the basis of this work. For any defect in printing or binding the publishers will be liable only to replace the defective copy by another copy of this work then available.

Written by

Parimal Ade & Gaurav Jain

Founders

InvestYadnya.in

Dedicated To

Indian Investors

Disclaimer

* All the examples mentioned in the book are chosen arbitrarily and we do not endorse any of the Mutual Fund schemes mentioned in the examples in anyway.

* We don't have any partnership, allegiance or love for any financial company, bank or financial products.

* We have taken the utmost care to keep the information completely unbiased.

* All the information such as returns, interest rate, expense ratio, Fund Portfolio etc. are in the reference to the 1st April 2023 data unless or until mentioned.

* All the NAVs, returns and expense ratio mentioned in the book are of Direct & Growth plans of mutual funds unless mentioned otherwise.

* All the company names, trade names, trademarks, designs, copyrights, products referenced in this book are the property of their respective owners. No company references in this book sponsored this book or the contents thereof.

* Although the author and publisher have made every effort to ensure that the information in this book was correct at press time, the author and publisher do not assume and hereby disclaim any liability to any party for any loss or damage caused by errors or omissions, whether such errors or omissions result from negligence, accident, or any other cause.

* This book is not intended as a substitute for the financial advice in any way. The reader should regularly consult a financial advisor in matters relating to his/her individual money needs.

* References are provided for informational purposes only and do not constitute endorsement of any websites or other sources.

* You should seek the services of a competent professional financial advisor before investing in Mutual Funds.

* Mutual Fund investments are Subject to Market Risk, always read the scheme related documents before investing.

Contents

Contents

Preface

In our work of leading Yadnya, our goal is to impart unbiased Investment education so that every Indian can take an informed decision about his/her money. In doing so, we talk to many investors: young, working and retired; low, medium and high income group; low, medium and high risk takers. Each one of them has continuously challenged us and inspired us to make money management simpler and easier.

Each day, I answer at least 50 questions on money management, which prompted me to write this first book on frequently asked and very relevant questions on one of the most popular investment option today – Mutual Funds. Mutual Fund industry in India has grown exponentially since entry of private players in early 1990s. Today, they manage more than ₹40 Lakh Crore worth of assets, which is increasing very rapidly!

Purpose of this book is to simplify how, what and why questions on Mutual Funds and the ones related to systematic transactions (SIP, STP, SWP etc.).

After reading this book, I am sure you will be able to take informed decisions on your investments, will be able to ask right questions to your investment advisor and will be able to understand all type of Mutual Funds in India. This book is India specific and all the information, rules and regulations are written keeping in mind only the Indian market.

I have updated this book due to many regulatory changes and fund house level changes. Few advance concepts in Mutual Funds are also introduced in this version.

I would like to thank Gaurav, co-author of this book who came up with this idea of a book to simplify the concepts for all. I am profoundly grateful to all my clients for asking all the relevant and difficult questions, which helped me to read & learn more.

I would also like to thank Ashwini and Manisha for reviewing, editing and improving the work and giving relevant suggestions.

Finally, I would like to thank my family for their support and patience during the process of writing this book.

Parimal Ade

April 2023

About Yadnya

The word Yadnya means a holy fire where oblations, chanting of hymns, and offerings are given. Yadnya contributes to the moral and spiritual upliftment of the society.

True to our name, we are offering our time, knowledge and focus to the holy fire of financial literacy in India. We are committed to the cause of financial upliftment of our society.

Mission

Our Mission is to educate and simplify concepts of personal finance for every Indian.

We don't have any partnership, allegiance or love for any financial company, bank or financial products. We are more neutral than cricket umpires. You can get completely unbiased and reason based coaching from us. Period!

What we offer?

We utilize multiple ways to spread knowledge and coach people about simple and impactful fundamentals of managing their own money-

1. YouTube Channel – *youtube.com/InvestYadnya* – One of the largest and fastest growing personal finance channel in India. In English and Hindi Language.

2. Financial Planning portal – https://investyadnya.in – Here you can create your Financial Plan for Free and get it reviewed by experts.

3. Mutual Fund Research Platform – Fund-o-meter. This platform is most comprehensive MF research & Rating platform in India.

4. Facebook Page – *facebook.com/InvestYadnya*

5. Twitter Handle – Twitter.com/InvestYadnya

6. Class room trainings on multiple topics – Introduction to Financial Concepts, Financial Planning, Retirement Planning, Insurance Planning, Tax Planning, Investment Options, Know your Salary and many more.

We are Yadnya

CATEGORY 1

Introduction To Mutual Funds

"A mutual fund can do for you what you would do for yourself if you had sufficient time, training, and money to diversify, plus the temperament to stand back from your money and make rational decisions."

–Venita VanCaspel

1.   WHAT IS A MUTUAL FUND?

Numerous individuals pooling in money with the sole intention of earning returns is called a mutual fund. Investing in Mutual Funds is normally much easier than buying or selling financial securities like stocks, bonds or money market instruments. Mutual funds are managed by professional 'fund managers' who invest the fund's capital in various financial securities based on the objective of the fund and attempt to produce capital gains and income for the fund's investors.

These Fund Managers are highly qualified individuals who invest your money based on a lot of backend research.

As a Mutual Fund investor, you own units of a Mutual Fund but not any securities directly. All the investors of a fund share in the fund's gains and losses proportional to the amount they've invested.

As a Mutual Fund investor, the biggest benefit you get is diversification. A Fund Manager will always hedge the risk by investing in many financial securities, which help in having a diversified portfolio. A typical Fund may have 20 – 100 number of securities in different quantities.

Each Mutual Fund has a different investment objective, which is set by Fund Manager before launching the Fund in the market. Based on this objective, the Fund Manager picks up financial securities for the fund and sets its return and risk expectation. *For example*, if the Fund objective is wealth conservation, then Fund Manager would invest most of the money in Debt and Liquid instruments, which are less risky and give inflation comparable returns.

Examples of few big Mutual Fund houses in India: ICICI Prudential Mutual Fund, HDFC Mutual Fund, Nippon Mutual Fund, SBI Mutual Fund, Aditya Birla Sun Life Mutual Fund, etc.

2. WHAT ARE ADVANTAGES AND DISADVANTAGES OF MUTUAL FUNDS?

8 Advantages of Mutual Funds:

1. Diversification: One of the primary goals of investment must be diversification of risk and Mutual Funds accomplish this goal well. With a single mutual fund, you invest into various assets and many corporations. If one stock or asset goes down, there are others that may compensate for it.

2. Expert Management: Mutual Fund managers are highly qualified and experienced professionals who are constantly researching, analysing and managing their funds. Mutual fund companies have access to information beyond what you as an individual or a retail investor have.

3. Liquidity: You can sell or buy mutual funds anytime. Mutual funds are good if you want to invest in an easy to liquidate instrument. Investments can be redeemed within 1-3 working days. More about this in Q113.

4. Convenience: Mutual Fund investments are highly convenient as you can invest through various channels (Demat Account, Online Bank Investment Account, Direct

through Mutual Fund houses, Mutual Fund distributors, various online investment platforms, etc.), can invest anytime, can invest in very small amounts (as low as ₹500), can easily track your portfolio (through mobile apps and monthly reports), get professional management without amateur intervention, access of investment in few financial securities such as Govt. securities, which you as an individual or retail investor do not have easy direct access to.

5. Reinvestment of Income: Mutual funds allow investors to reinvest their dividends and interest in additional fund units. This helps in timely investment of your dividends and interest giving a compounding effect.

6. Range of Investment Options and Objectives: You can find a mutual fund that matches almost exactly what you are looking for in an investment. This could be related to both your risk profile and your investment horizon. We will discuss this in detail in Q3.

7. Affordability: You can start your Mutual Fund investment with as low as ₹500. With that money, you could own assets of many corporations, which otherwise is not possible with such small amounts.

8. Transparency & Ease of Comparison: You can track your fund performance on daily basis and easily compare your Mutual fund with peers and benchmark to know their performance and accordingly take a call to invest more or to sell the existing one.

5 Disadvantages of Mutual Funds:

1. Exit Loads: Many of the Mutual Funds charge an Exit load, which means a penalty if you redeem your investments before a certain timeframe. Exit Load varies across fund schemes and can be as high as 2% of total redemption and can also be 0%. More details in Q107.

2. Management Fees/Expense Ratio: As the saying goes, 'There are no free lunches on Wall Street', same goes for Mutual Funds. A Mutual Fund charges a fee for managing your money. It is charged as percentage of assets under management. We will discuss this in detail in Q106.

3. Subject to Market Risks and No Guaranteed Returns: Even though different kind of Mutual Funds carry different risk profiles, but none of them give you Guaranteed Returns like Bank FDs, PPF etc. Returns depend on Stock market conditions for Equity based funds and on interest rate fluctuations for debt funds.

4. Too Many Options create confusion: There are more than 40 Mutual Fund houses with more than 3000 primary schemes. It is not an easy task to select the right fund scheme, looking at different types and complexities associated with them. Even after recent rationalization of schemes by SEBI (Based on SEBI circular on 6th Oct 2017 named 'Categorization and Rationalization of Mutual Fund Schemes'), things have simplified a little bit but not too much.

5. No Control: Investment in Mutual Fund doesn't give you any control over the choice of securities selected by Fund Manager. You must completely trust his/her judgement.

Our Take:

We believe Mutual Funds are the most transparent, efficient and convenient way of investment. Yes, there are risks involved and therefore you should do your research or talk to your financial advisor to select the best fund that suit your needs.

3. WHAT ARE THE TYPES OF MUTUAL FUNDS?

Mutual funds can be divided in different types depending upon various criterias.

* Firstly, depending upon the *fund schemes*, Mutual Funds are classified as:

    1. <u>Open Ended Funds</u>: The most popular type. These are funds in which you can enter or exit anytime. They are not time bound. More details in Q6 and Q13.

    2. <u>Close Ended Funds</u>: After the closure of an initial offer, new investors cannot enter, nor can existing investors exit till the term of the scheme ends. These funds are listed on stock exchange and you can sell fund units on it, but liquidity is very low. More details in Q11.

    3. <u>Interval Funds</u>: Very few such funds are present in Indian market. These funds combine the characteristics of both closed-end and open-ended funds. These do not permit regular buying and selling as these remain closed for most of the time but open for a time interval predefined by the fund, wherein units can be redeemed, or new units can be bought. Like Close ended funds, these too can be traded on the stock exchange.

* Depending upon *management of funds*, Mutual Funds are classified as:

    1. <u>Actively Managed Funds</u>: These are the funds, in which fund managers actively pick securities based on their own research and analysis. These funds are compared to benchmarks which are mostly popular indices. There are many top-rated fund managers who consistently deliver exceptional results. In India, most of the Mutual Fund investments are

done in Actively Managed funds as fund managers consistently beat the benchmark and create an Alpha (returns over and above the predicted ones).

2. <u>Passively Managed Funds</u>: These are funds in which fund managers replicate an index with the same stocks and in the same proportion. They are also called as Index Funds or ETFs. Here the fund manager tries to replicate the index performance with little tracking error as the fund is subject to inflows and outflows. These funds have lower expense ratio and are gaining popularity. More details in Q58.

* Depending upon the *assets invested* in, Mutual Funds are classified as:

1. <u>Debt Funds</u>: These types of Mutual Funds invest their assets only in Debt (Fixed Income) Instruments such as Corporate Bonds, Debentures, Govt. Securities, etc. Their overall risk profile is low. More details in Q26.

2. <u>Equity Funds</u>: Equity Funds invest their assets in Stock market. These are also known as Stock Funds. These are the highest risk Mutual Funds. More details in Q14.

3. <u>Liquid Category Funds</u>: These funds invest their assets in low maturity Money market instruments such as Treasury Bills, Certificate of Deposits, etc. which have maturities of 1 to 180 days. They are the least risky Mutual Fund type. More details in Q41.

4. <u>Hybrid Funds</u>: These funds invest their money in both Equity and Debt and other instruments too. Ratio varies from fund to fund. These funds are

medium risk type and give you the best of both equity and debt funds. More details in Q43.

* Depending upon *investment objective* of funds, Mutual Funds are classified as:

    1. <u>Growth Funds</u>: These are equity-based funds that invest primarily in Stock Markets. While picking stocks, these funds look for potential to grow faster than the others. The fund managers mostly invest in stocks that have low dividend yields and high growth potential.

    2. <u>Value Funds</u>: These are also Equity based funds that invest in undervalued stocks with a potential for appreciation, but such stocks are usually ignored by the investing community. It is a more conservative approach of investing. They invest typically in stocks with high dividend yield and low P/E ratio.

    3. <u>Income Funds</u>: These funds invest primarily in Debt instruments and will give you regular dividends/interest and are known for capital protection.

* Some of the *special funds* are:

    1. <u>Index Funds</u>: Index funds closely follow the stock indices they track. For instance, a scheme that tracks the Sensex will invest in the 30 stocks that comprise the benchmark index of the BSE. These are a type of Passively Managed Funds. More details in Q62.

    2. <u>ETFs</u>: They are essentially Index Funds that are listed and traded on exchanges just like stocks. Another type of Passively Managed Funds. More Details in Q58.

    3. <u>Sectoral/Thematic Funds</u>: These are a type of Equity Funds, which invest their assets only in one focused sector/theme. Some popular sector funds are in

Banking, Technology, Pharma and Infrastructure sector. More Details in Q55.

4. <u>Tax Saving Funds</u>: Also, known as ELSS, they are a type of Equity funds, which have 3 years lock in and your investments get tax benefit under Section 80C. More details in Q68.

5. <u>International Funds</u>: These mutual funds invest in companies outside India. They help you to invest and get an exposure to Global companies. More details in Q77.

6. <u>Retirement/Children Funds</u>: These are solution oriented Mutual Funds in new SEBI categorization and have a 5-year lock in. More details in Q80.

4. WHAT IS NET ASSET VALUE? HOW IT IS CALCULATED?

Net asset value (NAV) is a mutual fund's price per unit. In other words, it is the value of a single unit of a mutual fund.

$$NAV = \frac{[Total\ Value\ of\ stocks,\ bonds\ held\ by\ Mutual\ Fund\ (Total\ Assets) - Daily\ Expenses\ (Total\ Liabilities)]}{Total\ Number\ of\ Units}$$

It changes once every working day as the value of the bonds, deposits and stocks the fund holds, changes every working day; except ETF, where the NAV changes real time with the change in markets. It is calculated by dividing the total value of all the securities in its portfolio, minus any liabilities (expense ratio), divided by the total number of units of the mutual fund.

Example:

On 1st Jan 2023, NAV of ICICI Prudential Equity & Debt Fund (Growth) was ₹243.07.

NAV of HDFC Top 100 Fund (Growth) was ₹930.01.

5. ARE INVESTMENTS IN MUTUAL FUNDS SAFE?

Risk profile of a Mutual Fund depends upon the following factors:

1. Majorly on the risk type of instruments they have invested in. For example: Stocks are relatively riskier than debt instruments like Bonds, Debentures, etc. Money market instruments (T-Bills, Commercial Papers, Certificate of Deposits, CBLO etc) with short maturity period are least risky instruments.

2. It also depends upon a lot of other factors such as

    a. Timing of investment – Is it a volatile market or a stable market?

    b. Quality of assets chosen – Chance of their bad performance during holding period

    c. Govt. Policy – Is the current government pro-industry or not? Are they reforming the economy well?

    d. Country's economy – How is the economy performing? Economy growth? Liquidity? Competition etc.

    e. External Factors – Global Financial markets, Geo-Political landscape etc.

Mutual fund returns depend upon the market value of the assets, which is impacted by the above-mentioned factors. However, these investments are highly secured from any kind of fraud. Heavy government regulations and a market regulator like SEBI manages the privacy and safety aspects very closely. For Examples SEBI imposed high penalty on ICICI Pru Mutual Fund for investing their fund's money in their parent company's new IPO (ICICI Securities). A similar high penalty was imposed on HDFC Mutual Fund for doing private placement for some of their shares to their top mutual fund distributors before IPO launch.

6. HOW LIQUID ARE MUTUAL FUNDS?

Investments in Mutual Funds are highly liquid. The degree of liquidity differs though; this difference depends upon the type of scheme you invest in:

1. <u>Open Ended Funds</u> – Most popular ones, it is a type of Mutual Fund that issues and redeems units at any time. There is continuous buying and selling of units of such funds with the mutual fund house. An investor can redeem his/her investment, whenever he/she wants. After redemption, money is credited to the account within 1-4 working days based on type of fund. If redeemed within a specific holding period, many of the Open-Ended Funds levy an Exit Load, which can range from 0% to 2%. This is done to prevent investors from redeeming their investments very early in the scheme. Please do check these penalties before redeeming your investments. There is no lock-in in these funds. (More details in Q13)

2. <u>Closed Ended Schemes</u> – It is a type of Mutual Fund that issues a fixed number of units in the market. Investors cannot buy units of closed end funds after its NFO (New Fund Offer) is over. If the closed ended funds are listed in any stock exchange, then these can be traded but liquidity/volume for these funds is very low and therefore are difficult to exit.

7. GROWTH v/s DIVIDEND OPTION v/s DIVIDEND RE-INVESTMENT OPTION?

<u>Growth Option:</u>

Under this option, you will not receive any returns in the intermediate time. You will not receive any payment in the form of interest, dividends, gains, bonus, etc. You will get your returns only after selling the units.

Example:

You bought 100 units of a mutual fund scheme at a NAV of ₹20 and you sold those units after 5 years when the NAV had reached ₹100. So, your returns will be ₹10000 (100*₹100) – 2000 (100* ₹20) = ₹8000. You will not get any pay-out in between.

Tax Applicability:

Only Capital Gain tax is applicable.

For Equity funds (if Equity allocation is more than 65%): Capital gains redeemed within 1 year would be taxed at 15% flat and there would be 10% tax on the ones redeemed after a year. More Details in Q19.

For Hybrid Funds (if Equity allocation is less than 65% but more than 35%): On investments redeemed within 3 years, you are liable to pay taxes on the gains as per your tax slab and on the ones redeemed after 3 years, you are liable to pay taxes on the gains at 20% flat but after Indexation.

For Debt Funds (if Equity allocation is less than 35%): You are liable to pay taxes on the gains as per your tax slab.

<u>Dividend Option:</u>

Now known as "Payout of Income Distribution cum Capital withdrawal (P-IDCW) option"

Under this option, you will receive returns in the intermediate time . However, Dividend amount is not fixed.

Equity Funds do not give regular Dividends. Debt Funds may give you an option of daily/ weekly/ monthly/ quarterly dividend pay-out.

Example:

You have invested in a mutual fund at NAV of ₹20 with dividend option. The scheme performs well and NAV reaches a level of ₹30. The fund house may decide to pay out ₹2/unit as dividend.

So, you receive ₹2/unit in between and simultaneously the NAV will fall to ₹28.

Tax Applicability:

Tax applicability on the capital gains made on investment is same as growth option. Dividends are taxed as per your tax slab. Earlier Dividend Distribution Tax (DDT) was deducted by Mutual Fund houses but DDT was abolished in Budget 2020. So you can choose this option if you are in 0%, 5% or 10% tax slab.

Dividend Re-Investment Option:

Now known as 'Reinvestment of Income distribution cum capital withdrawal plan (R-IDCW)'

It is a combination of both growth and dividend options. Basically, the fund declares dividend, but despite issuing the dividend in the form of cash, it re-invests the dividend into the same scheme for additional units.

Example:

You bought 100 units of a mutual fund scheme at a NAV of ₹20 and after 1 year, fund's NAV rises to ₹30 and a dividend of ₹2/unit is declared. Now, the new NAV would be ₹28 and the dividend of ₹200 (₹2*100) would be reinvested at a NAV of ₹28. You would get almost 7 (₹200/₹28) additional units. Therefore, you would have 107 units at NAV ₹28 and you would not get any cash pay-out due to the reinvestment.

Tax Applicability:

Tax applicability on the gains made on redemption of investment is same as growth option. And in case of dividends declared & re-invested, tax treatment is same as that of dividend option. So, you have paid tax every time dividend is declared and re-invested whereas in Growth option, tax needs to be paid only when there is redemption. Dividend Re-investment option is an inefficient Growth option. Growth is always better than Dividend Re-investment.

Basis	Growth Option	Dividend Option (P-IDCW)	Dividend Re-Investment (R-IDCW)
Profit Actions	Profits are not paid directly to investors; they are reinvested and the lump sum amount is paid at the end.	Profits are stripped out of your NAV and given to you periodically.	Same as Growth Option
Effect of compounding	As the profits are reinvested immediately, there's a benefit of compounding on returns until the maturity period.	A part of the profit is paid out, so compounding effect is not at its full potential	Same as Growth Option
Choice suits	The investors targeting for long term financial goals and looking for long term investment plans should opt for growth option.	It only suits investors who are in low income tax slab like 0%, 5% or 10%.	Growth is better in every way. If you want regular income, go for SWP.
Taxation	Only Capital Gain Tax	* Capital Gains Tax on gains on redemption * Dividends are taxed as per your tax slab * 10% TDS if dividends are more than Rs 5000	Same as Dividend Option

Our Take:

* If you are unsure of when you will redeem, choose *growth* option

* If you are investing in Equity Funds, choose *growth* option

* Choose Dividend option only if you have regular money requirement, are in a 0%, 5% or 10% tax bracket
* If you still do not understand the difference, choose *growth* option

The problem with Mutual Fund dividends is that they are not purely dividends. To the investor, word 'dividend' means corporate dividends, which are indicative of how profitable a company is and how much profits are being distributed to shareholders. In funds, dividends are not like that, instead, they are a withdrawal from your own account. This the reason SEBI changed the Dividend Plan names in Oct 2020. The purpose of this move is to communicate to investors that in case of equity shares dividend is a distribution of profits by a corporation to its shareholders, but in the case of mutual fund units it is paid out from your own capital.

8.   CAN NRI INVEST IN MUTUAL FUNDS IN INDIA?

YES, NRIs can invest in Mutual Funds in India. Investments can be made on repatriable (taking back assets outside India) basis or non-repatriable basis.

To invest on a repatriable basis: It refers to the investment wherein NRI can take the invested money back in foreign currency. NRI must have an NRE account with a bank in India.

To invest on a non-repatriable basis: It refers to the investment wherein NRI cannot convert invested money back to his home country. For this purpose, NRI must have an NRO account.

An NRI cannot make investments in foreign currency. The tax liability of the NRI is the same as an Indian Resident but TDS is applicable for NRI investments at the highest applicable slab for that investment. TDS needs to be deducted by Mutual Fund house. Please remember TDS is not applicable for Resident Indians.

Please note: Local laws in some countries such as the US and Canada restrict investment by their residents. Due to laws under FATCA, there is a complexity associated with the compliance. Few mutual funds do not accept investments from Canada & US NRIs and many others accept it with additional documentations such as declaration signed by NRIs. NRI from the Middle East, Singapore, Hong Kong, UK or Europe are free to invest in any mutual fund scheme.

9. WHAT ARE NFOs?

NFO stands for New Fund Offer, under which a First-Time offer is made by the mutual fund house, to newly introduce a mutual fund in the market. A new fund offer is launched in the market to raise capital from the public to buy securities like shares, govt. bonds, etc. from the market.

NFO and IPO (Initial Public Offering) might seem similar terms, however they are different. The main difference is that through IPOs direct stocks of a company are launched and through NFOs new Mutual funds are launched in the market. NFOs are sold on the Net asset value whereas IPOs offer stocks on the stock price. NFOs can be open ended or closed ended.

For Example:

Parag Parikh Conservative Hybrid Fund(G) (An Open Ended Equity Scheme) was open for subscription on 7th May, 2021.

10. SHOULD I INVEST IN NFOS?

Are NFOs cheaper?

Yes, for Closed End Funds (FMPs etc.). Closed Ended Funds are offered only through NFOs, so if you want to invest in products like FMPs, then you should invest in NFOs. We will discuss about Closed Ended Funds in Q11.

<u>May be, for Passively Managed Funds</u>. If any new ETF is getting launched, which has lower expense ratio than existing or is tracking a new asset like REITs, international index, or commodities like silver for which there are limited existing investment options, then you may opt for such NFOs based on your preferences.

<u>Absolutely NO for Open Ended Actively Managed Funds</u>. Even if there is an NFO, you should avoid investing in such schemes due to following reasons:

1. They have no proven track record.

2. Most of the times such funds come with higher Expense ratio as their initial marketing cost etc. is higher.

3. They are not cheaper than already existing funds. This is a myth that ₹10 NFOs are cheaper than their existing peers as the NAV of the later would be higher and hence lesser units would be bought for the same cost. This is totally wrong. Your returns depend only on the percentage growth on NAV, based on the portfolio of that fund. So hypothetically, if there are two funds with exactly same stock portfolio A & B. A is an NFO with NAV of ₹10 whereas B has been in the market for 10 years and has NAV of ₹200. Then if underlying portfolio increases by 10% in a year, then NAV of A will become ₹11 and NAV of B will become ₹220. So, no difference in returns.

4. NFOs are not like IPOs: In NFO the NAV is fixed and is not affected due to the demand or other factors. While in IPO the listing price of the stock depends on the demand and market's expectation of the company.

5. During most of the times, NFO is launched when the underlying sector/category is already at the top of its returns cycle which makes it more popular to invest in.

11. WHAT ARE CLOSED ENDED FUNDS?

Close-ended mutual fund Schemes have a fixed maturity period wherein you can invest directly in the scheme at the time of the initial issue and thereafter if the scheme is listed, units of the scheme can be bought or sold on the stock exchange. All closed ended funds are required to be listed on stock exchange so that investors have a window to exit in between as well. But liquidity of these funds is mostly very low at exchange.

Few Examples:

Fund Name	Type	Launch Date	Duration (Lock In)
ICICI Prudential R.I.G.H.T Fund	ELSS	Sep 2009	10 years
SBI Tax Advantage Fund – Series I	ELSS	Mar 2008	10 Years
Canara Robeco Capital Protection Oriented Fund Series 10	Hybrid	Mar 2019	3 Years
SBI FMP Series 41 (1498 Days)	Debt	May 2021	4 Years

12. SHOULD I INVEST IN CLOSED ENDED FUNDS?

Basically, the investment in open ended funds is flexible as the time and the manner of buying these funds are easy whereas there is lesser flexibility in case of closed end funds.

It is difficult to generalize whether open ended funds are better than closed end funds or vice versa. The performance of a fund, whether open ended or closed ended, depends on the fund management, investment style and the fund category.

Why you should invest?

1. Investment lock in helps in staying invested and avoiding impulse redemption of the funds.

2. Lock in also helps Fund Manager to take long term growth potential calls. Stable Asset Under Management also helps them to manage the money more efficiently.

3. In Debt Closed Ended funds – Lock-in helps in predictable returns when there are very low interest rate fluctuations

Why you shouldn't?

1. No past record in NFO and therefore difficult to set a selection criterion.

2. It doesn't allow Systematic Investments (SIP, STP, SWP etc.).

3. Low flexibility – Difficult to exit before maturity, as there is very low liquidity on stock exchange for these funds.

4. Mostly best fund managers do not manage Closed ended schemes due to low AUMs

You should invest in these funds based on the kind of investor you are. If you are a disciplined investor and work on asset allocation concept, then prefer to invest in open ended funds only.

Whereas if you are an impulsive investor and track market very closely but do not have short term requirements, you should prefer closed ended funds for some percentage of your investment, to lock and forget.

13. CLOSED ENDED V/S OPEN ENDED MUTUAL FUNDS?

Basis	Closed Ended Funds	Open Ended Funds
No of units outstanding	Fixed based on amount initially invested	Can issue units regularly based on demand
Term	Difficult to exit before the end of term of the scheme	There are no entry-exit restrictions
Units to be sold	The number of units to be sold are fixed	There is no such restriction regarding number of units to be sold
Timing	You can enter only in a small window of time, open during NFO	You can invest anytime and chose your own investment duration
Popularity	Less popular and holds about 12% assets of Mutual Funds	Much more popular and holds about 88% assets of Mutual Funds

CATEGORY 2

Equity Mutual Funds

"If you have the stomach for stocks, but neither the time nor the inclination to do the homework, invest in equity mutual funds."

–Peter Lynch

14. WHAT IS AN EQUITY MUTUAL FUND?

Equity mutual funds are mutual funds, which primarily invest in stocks to get the benefit from rising stock prices in the capital market. The returns on equity mutual funds are in the form of dividends as well as capital gains. Equity funds give an investor indirect ownership in the company, wherein unlike debentures one does not get just a fixed interest.

Investments in Equity funds should be done for long term goals such as retirement, child education etc. as mostly these funds can be highly volatile if held for a short duration.

Equity Mutual Funds (Including Tax Saving category) have about 1/3rd of the total Asset under management in Indian Mutual Fund market. There are wide choices before investors, with about 500 schemes to choose from.

Example:

Kotak Flexicap Fund is currently the biggest Active Equity Fund with assets under management of close to ₹37k Crores in Indian market and has given approximately 13.58% returns per annum since launch in the last 10 years. (as of Jan 2023)

15. SHOULD I INVEST IN EQUITY MUTUAL FUNDS?

Equity Funds Pros and Cons

YES, you should invest in Equity Mutual Funds for all your long term financial goals such as Retirement, Child's education, Child's Marriage or any other goal which is atleast 5 years away. Following are advantages and disadvantages of investing in Equity Mutual Funds

Advantages of Equity Mutual Fund

i. Diversification: Equity Mutual Funds give you an automatic diversification in many different stocks. **Example**, Large cap funds generally have 40-60 stocks in its portfolio.

ii.   Liquidity: Equity Funds are reasonably liquid with money getting credited in your bank account within 3-4 working days after redemption. Though few funds charge an exit load, of as high as 2% if you redeem investment before a stipulated period (mostly 1 year). **Example:** Kotak Flexicap charges an exit load of 1% on 90% of the amount if investment is redeemed in first 365 days. There is no load on redemption on first 10% of the amount (as of 24th May 2022).

iii. Professional Management: Money invested in equity markets is managed professionally by fund managers, many of them regularly beat their fund's benchmarks.

iv.   Can Start Small: You can start your investment with as low as ₹5000 as lumpsum and ₹500 as SIP and can own big basket of stocks.

v.   Exceptional Past Returns: In last 10 years, diversified Equity Funds have given an average of close to 14% per annum returns (as on Jan 24, 2023)

Disadvantages of Equity Mutual Fund

i.   Not for Short term: Equity funds can't be an investment option for short term as the returns are very volatile for short period.

ii.   No Control: Investor has no control over his/her investments as all the decisions are taken by the fund manager.

iii. Cost: There are fees associated with investment in mutual funds. **Example:** HDFC Equity Savings Fund has an expense ratio of 2.04% and also exit load of 1% on 85% of the amount if redeemed within first 3 months.

iv.   Choice Overload: There are over 600 schemes of Equity Mutual Funds to choose from, with many different objectives. You should always talk to your advisor before finalizing the scheme.

16. DIRECT STOCK INVESTING VS EQUITY MUTUAL FUNDS

A common question many investors ask is, why not direct stock investing instead of Mutual Funds? Many argue that Direct stock investing is more exciting and this adrenaline driven investment option gives flexibility to easily emulate portfolios of the likes of Rakesh Jhunjhunwala or a star fund manager, then why people recommend Equity Funds.

We believe answer lies in your current stock portfolio. Simply compare your overall last 5 year returns from your direct stock portfolio with any of the average performer Equity Fund and if your returns are better or even at par, then direct stock investing is for you otherwise sell everything and buy Equity Funds. Let's understand the difference better in detail:

Basis	Direct Equity	Equity Mutual Funds
Diversification	Biggest risk with direct equity is lack of diversification. Investing in few stocks or companies of 1-2 sectors can lead to high losses	1 Unit of Equity Fund gives you diversification to more than 20-30 stocks
Research & Management	You need to do your own research and portfolio management to know right time to buy and sell	A professional team of fund manager and Analysts do it for you. Much lesser effort for you
Risk	Riskier than Equity Funds majorly due to lack of diversification and lack of expertise	Less risky than Direct Equity due to better management
Entry Level	Just buying 1 stock each of Sensex companies would require you to invest more than ₹75,000 (as of 31ˢᵗ Dec 2022)	Here you can buy a Sensex ETF for as low as ₹500

Cost	Your direct equity cost can be higher or lesser in short term than Equity fund based on your brokerage plan. It mostly turns out to be lower if you hold the scrip for long.	Regular Equity Funds charge an expense ratio between 1.0-2.5% per annum on your portfolio. Lower cost option – ETF/Index Funds which charge as low as 0.05% per annum or Direct MF plans which charge less than 1% are available too
Mode of Investment	Only through Demat account	Many options – Demat account or Mutual Fund account directly held with Fund house or various online portals. Details in Q102.
Systematic Investments	Very hard to implement SIP, STP & SWP type of investments here	Very easy/automatic route to do systematic investments

Our Take:

Direct Equity investing is strictly for investors who have the time to actively monitor and research stocks, have a reasonable knowledge about the financial markets and have the patience to bear market volatility. If you do not satisfy any of the above conditions, go for Equity Mutual Funds.

17. WHAT ARE THE TYPES OF EQUITY MUTUAL FUNDS?

SEBI in its circular dated 6th Oct 2017 named 'Categorization & Rationalization of Mutual Fund Schemes' has clearly defined the categories of all Mutual Funds. They have mandated that each fund house will only have maximum 1 fund in each category now (except Sector/thematic category). Due to this, there were lot of changes – new names of old schemes, mergers of few schemes and re-categorization of few schemes etc. which happened in Apr/May 2018. Following diagram shows the Equity Mutual Fund categories defined by SEBI

Multi Cap Fund	Large Cap Fund	Large & Mid Cap Fund	Mid Cap Fund	Small Cap Fund
Min 25% in Large Cap Min 25% in Mid Cap Min 25 in Small Cap	Min 80% in Large Cap	Min 35% in large Cap Min 35% in Mid Caps	Min 65% in Mid Caps	Min 65% in Small Caps
Flexi Cap Fund	**ELSS**	**Value Fund/ Contra Fund**	**Focused Fund**	**Dividend Yield Fund**
Min 65% in Equity Invest across Large, Mid, Small	Min 80% in Equity assets	Value/Contrarian Investment strategy	Max 30 Stocks in portfolio	Pre-dominantly in Dividend Yielding Stocks

Following table gives the details about types of Equity Mutual Funds based on SEBI's mandate –

Type of Equity Mutual Fund	Description	Examples
Large Cap Funds	Large Cap Companies are defined as Top 100 Companies by market Cap listed in the recognized stock exchanges in India. Large Cap Funds have to invest a minimum of 80% of their total assets in the large cap companies.	Aditya Birla Sunlife Frontline Equity, SBI Blue Chip Fund, Axis Bluechip Fund, etc.
Mid Cap Funds	Mid Cap companies are defined as Top 101st – 250th companies by market Cap listed in the recognized stock exchanges in India. Mid Cap Funds have to invest a minimum of 65% of their total assets in such Mid cap companies.	HDFC Mid-Cap Opportunities, Sundaram Mid Cap Fund, UTI Midcap Fund, etc.
Small Cap Funds	Small Cap companies are defined as 251st company onwards in terms of market capitalization. Small Cap Funds have to invest a minimum of 65% of their total assets in such Small cap companies.	DSP Small Cap Fund, Franklin India Smaller Companies Fund, etc.

Flexi Cap Funds	These funds do not restrict themselves based on Market Cap of the company and can invest in any stock across Large, Mid & Small Cap. Earlier this category was known as Multi Cap Category but name change was done by SEBI in Nov 2020. Multi cap category still exists and definition is as below.	HDFC Flexi Cap, IDFC Flexi Cap Fund, Franklin India Flexi Cap, etc.
Multi Cap Funds	This category was re-defined by SEBI in Sept 2020 – these funds are now mandated to invest minimum 25% of assets in Large Cap Stocks, 25% in Mid Cap Stocks, and 25% in Small Cap Stocks. Rest 25%, they can invest anywhere.	Nippon India Multi Cap Fund, Mahindra Manulife Multi Cap Badhat Yojana, ICICI Pru Multi Cap Fund etc.
Large & Mid Cap Funds	In this category, fund is mandated to invest a minimum of 35% of assets in Large Cap Stocks and 35% in Mid Cap Stocks. Rest they can invest anywhere.	Tata Large & Mid Cap Fund, Mirae Asset Emerging Bluechip Fund, etc.
Tax Saving (ELSS)	These are Flexi Cap funds with a 3-years lock-in and give Tax benefit under Sec 80C. They can invest in any stock across Large, Mid & Small Cap	Axis Long Term Equity Fund, HSBC Tax Saver Equity Fund, etc.
Contra/Value Funds	These are Flexi cap funds but follow a contrarian or value investing strategy. To know more about them, see Q24	ICICI Prudential Value Discovery Fund, Invesco India Contra Fund, etc.

Contd.

Focused Funds	These are Flexi cap funds but focused on fewer number of stocks (maximum 30)	SBI Focused Equity Fund, IDFC Focused Equity Fund, etc.
Dividend Yield Funds	These are multi cap funds which invest pre-dominantly in high dividend yielding stocks	UTI Dividend Yield Fund, Aditya Birla SL Dividend Yield Fund, etc.
Sector Funds	These Equity Funds invest only in a specific sector – FMCG, Banking, Infra, Pharma, etc. They have to invest a minimum of 80% of total assets into that particular sector.	UTI Infrastructure Fund, Nippon India Banking Fund, etc.
Thematic Funds	These Equity Funds can invest in any specific theme such as only MNC stocks, only consumer driven companies' stocks, only companies with reach in Rural India etc. They have to invest a minimum of 80% of total assets into stocks of that particular theme.	Aditya Birla Sunlife MNC Fund, Sundaram Rural & Consumption Fund, Invesco India ESG Fund etc.
International Funds	These invest in stocks of global companies listed outside India. For details, check Q77.	ICICI Prudential US Bluechip Equity Fund, Franklin Asian Equity Fund, etc.

More details on each of these types in upcoming answers.

18. IN GENERAL, HOW MANY EQUITY MUTUAL FUNDS SHOULD I OWN?

Diversification is the biggest advantage of investing in Equity Mutual Funds. You should invest in more than one Equity Fund only to diversify your risk of investing all your money with one Fund Manager. But please remember, too much diversification also doesn't help much, as many fund portfolios have high overlap.

You should buy mutual funds based on your investment objective, risk handling capacity and amount you are looking to invest. Generally, 5 to 7 different Mutual funds should be enough – a) Maximum 3 Flexi Cap/Small/Mid Cap Funds for very long term goals (>8 years), b) Maximum 2 Large Cap funds for Long Term Goals (>5 Years), c) 1-2 ELSS funds for your tax saving.

19. HOW ARE EQUITY FUNDS TAXED?

Capital Gain & Dividend taxation

Funds where equity holding is more than 65% of the total portfolio are classified as equity funds for taxation. All equity schemes, arbitrage funds, aggressive hybrid funds & Equity savings funds are classified as equity oriented funds from a taxation perspective.

Equity Oriented Mutual Funds –Tax Rate				
Type of security	Cut Off Date	Short Term Capital Gains (STCG Tax Rate)	Long Term Capital Gains (LTCG Tax Rate)	Dividend Tax
Equity Oriented Mutual Funds	Gains made till 31.01.2018	15%	Nil	As per Tax Slab (DDT Abolished in Feb 2020 budget)
	Gains made till 31.01.2018	15%	10% (For gains greater than ₹1 lakh)	

STCG – units held for less than 1 year, LTCG – units held for more than 1 year)

If you redeem your investments before 12 months, there is a flat 15 per cent capital gains tax on your gains, no matter which tax bracket you belong to.

Till FY 2017-18 Equity-oriented funds had no tax on long-term capital gains; i.e., if you sell your fund after 12 months from the date you bought them, you didn't had to pay any tax on your gains. But things changed after budget 2018, Finance minister introduced long term capital gains tax (LTCG) on sale of listed securities and Equity Mutual Funds.

Long-term capital gains tax of 10 percent was introduced on Equities. In the year of redemption, the gains that exceed ₹1 Lakh would be taxed at 10%. However, all gains till 31st January 2018 would be grandfathered.

If you have long term gains/profits before 31st Jan 2018, then you don't have to pay taxes on them. For this Finance Minister had used the term 'grandfathered' for gains earned before 31st Jan 2018. So, this tax is not retrospective. You have to pay tax only on gains you earn from 1st Feb 2018 onwards.

Here are various scenarios -

	Scenario 1	Scenario 2	Scenario 3	Scenario 4	Scenario 5
Purchase Date:	10 Jan 2018	10 Jan 2018	10 May 2017	10 Mar 2018	15 Jan 2017
Mutual Fund Purchase Price (₹)	1,00,000	1,00,000	1,00,000	1,00,000	1,00,000
Value as on 31st Jan. 2018 (₹)	1,20,000	1,20,000	1,75,000	NA	1,20,000
Redemption Date:	20 June 2019	20 June 2019	10 April 2018	10 June 2019	26 March 2018
Redemption Value (₹)	2,00,000	3,00,000	1,50,000	1,60,000	4,00,000
Fair Purchase Price (₹)	1,20,000	1,20,000	1,00,000	1,00,000	1,20,000
Capital Gains on Sale (₹)	80,000	1,80,000	50,000	60,000	2,80,000
STCG Tax (₹)	NA	NA	7,500 (15% on ₹50,000)	NA	NA
LTCG Tax (₹)	Nil (Total gains less than ₹1 lakh)	8,000 10% on (on 1.8 lakh - 1 lakh)	NA	NA (LTCG < 1 lakh)	No tax payable as the amendment is with effect from 01.04.2018

Here is how LTCG tax on Equity MF is calculated –

1. First, you should calculate cost of acquisition or Fair purchase price.

    The cost of acquisition of the MF unit bought before Feb 1, 2018, will be the higher of:

    a) the actual cost of acquisition of the MF

    b) The lower of: (i) The fair market value of MF (NAV of MF unit on 31.01.2018) and (ii) The sale value received/accrued when the share/unit is sold.

2. Calculate LTCG - For shares or equity MF units bought after 31.1.2018, capital gain would be computed as = Selling price - actual cost of acquisition (without indexation)

3. This LTCG will be taxed at 10% for the amount of more than ₹1 lakh per annum.

4. Please note – Capital Gains are taxed only in the Financial Year when you have redeemed your investments. So, if you invested in 2017-18 but redeemed your equity investments in 2021-22, then ₹1 lakh from those gains will be deducted before calculating LTCG tax in FY 2021-22. No tax benefit of ₹1 lakh will be given in the year 2018-19, 2019-20 or 2020-21 in this case and neither will this benefit gets carry forward.

All the dividends on mutual funds are now taxed as per you Income tax slab.

20. WHAT ARE LARGE CAP FUNDS? SHOULD I INVEST IN THEM?

Large cap funds are funds which invest atleast 80% of their total assets in equity and equity related instruments of Large cap companies. Large cap companies are top 100 companies by market cap listed on Indian stock exchanges. Large cap funds are safest when it comes to pure equity investing, easy to understand, less volatile to market swings and have predictable returns.

Examples of few Large Cap Funds- Aditya Birla Sun Life Frontline Fund, ICICI Prudential Bluechip, SBI Blue Chip Fund, etc.

Pros of Large Cap Funds

* Safest Equity Funds: Large cap funds are safer investment options as large-caps have the size and scale to weather the bad market phase and give stable returns

* Easier to track: Since large cap funds invest mostly in top companies which are most discussed and tracked companies in India, it is easier to evaluate and compare their performance

* Lower Expense ratio: Expense ratio of large cap funds is mostly less than other type of Equity Mutual Funds

* Good dividends: Since large cap companies are more mature, they tend to distribute their profits as dividends

Cons of Large Cap Funds

Not Exceptional Returns: Major flipside is that their returns are more predictable and not exceptional like mid cap/small cap funds. As of 24th Jan 2023, average 10 years returns of large cap funds is around 12.18% whereas it is more than 18% for small and mid-caps.

Our Take: Large Cap funds should be the core of your investment portfolio as they give stable and mostly inflation beating returns in the long term. You should tag your long-term goals (5-7 years) to these funds.

21.   WHAT ARE SMALL CAP & MID CAP FUNDS? SHOULD I INVEST IN THEM?

The small cap and mid-cap funds denote the size of companies these funds invest in; wherein cap is nothing but market capitalization of the company. Small cap funds are basically funds, which invest in companies that are in early stages of development. As per SEBI definition, they are the companies which are not in top 250 companies in India (in terms of market cap). In case of mid cap funds, the companies in which a fund invests are the top 101st to 250th companies by market cap in India (in terms of market cap). These represent mid-sized companies. While small and mid-caps have higher growth potential than large caps, such companies are more volatile and hence risky. However, quality small & mid-caps can prove to be efficient long term investments.

Examples of Small Cap & Mid Cap Funds: Franklin India Prima Fund, Sundaram Small Cap Fund, HSBC Mid-Cap Fund

There is no doubt that Small Cap and Mid-Cap funds are one of the riskiest Mutual Funds, but then with higher risk come higher returns. Let's find advantages and disadvantages of investing in such funds for you –

Pros of Small Cap & Mid Cap Funds

*	Good Returns in last few years: Small and mid-cap funds have given amazing returns in last few years. Last 10 years'

average returns of such funds are more than 18% p.a. as of 24th Jan 2023.

* Higher Growth potential: Though these funds invest into companies having lesser market cap than large cap companies, these small companies have the potential to be future large cap companies and hence can generate higher returns. Skill is to identify the right ones.

* Higher dependence on expertise: It is all about picking the right stock to make bountiful returns in Small and Mid-cap market. So, mutual funds do that for you by using the best talent in the industry.

Cons of Small & Mid Cap Funds

* Though there is room for growth, future of small and mid-cap companies is unpredictable and uncertain too depending upon market conditions

* As these funds invest in small and mid-cap companies, they are very volatile. There is also a higher risk of company becoming bankrupt as compared to large cap companies. Example – In 2018, returns of average Small Cap Fund was (-)17.25% whereas it is 1.64% for large caps.

* Small & Mid cap companies' growth is also dependent on interest rate scenario. So, any change in interest rate impacts their loan sheets, which can spur or reduce growth based on the direction of the interest rate movement. This impact is negligible in large caps due to their very high revenue numbers.

Our Take:

Small & Mid Cap fund performance in last few years has surpassed Sensex returns by a good margin. Also, options of such funds have increased recently. We would recommend you to invest in good small cap and mid cap funds for your very long term goals (>10 years).

22. SHOULD I OPT FOR FLEXI CAP, MULTI CAP OR LARGE & MID CAP CATEGORY?

Large & Mid Cap was a category defined in SEBI's guideline of 2017. There was no formal or informal category by this name before. Large & Mid Cap is defined as the category in which a fund has to allocate a min 35% of assets to Large Caps and a min 35% to Mid Cap stocks. Many large and good performing funds have categorized themselves into this category such as Mirae Asset Emerging Bluechip Fund (which was mostly tagged as mid cap before), Nippon India Vision Fund (which was tagged as Large Cap before) etc.

Whereas Flexi Cap (Known as Multi Cap before Sept 2021) is an old category where fund manager has complete freedom to allocate funds in stocks across market capitalisations. In this category, there is no restriction on minimum allocation to large, mid or small cap stocks. Fund can take 0 to 100% allocation in any Large, Mid or Small Cap category. There are already some big funds settled in this category such as HDFC Flexi Cap Fund, Franklin India Flexi Cap Fund (earlier known as Franklin India Equity Fund), Kotak Flexi Cap Fund (earlier known as Kotak Standard Multicap Fund) etc.

Multi Cap is a newly introduced category in Sept 2020 by SEBI. In this category, fund has to allocate a min 25% to Large Caps, min 25% to Mid Cap stocks and min 25% in Small Cap Stocks. Since it is a new category, there are limited options of investment currently. Few big funds which are in this category are Nippon India Multi Cap Fund and ICICI Pru Multi Cap Fund.

Each category has their own Pros & Cons –

Basis	Large & Mid Cap	Flexi Cap	Multi Cap
Definition	Funds with min 35% in Large Caps and min 35% in Mid-Caps	Can invest in stocks of any capitalisation as they want. No restriction.	Funds with min 25% in Large Caps, min 25% in Mid-Caps and 25% in Small Caps
Risk	Little lower as compared to Multi Caps. Due to allocation restrictions, investors know what they are investing into.	Higher Risk as Fund manager can invest anywhere. Each fund in the category could have very different allocation based on Fund Manager's view of the market.	Little higher risk than large & midcap as there is a restriction to buy min. 50% small & midcap stocks, but investors do know what they are investing into
Fits	This category fits better for investor who can afford higher risk than Large Caps. Good for goals 7+ Years away.	This category fits who trust their Fund Managers. They know fund manager will take the right call on allocations based on market conditions. Also, good for goals 7+ Years away.	This category fits investor who wants a real multicap fund with compulsory representation of all different market caps and need to manage their asset allocation accordingly
Returns	Very close categories in terms of profile. Should have similar return in the long term.		

Our Take: Large & Mid Cap is a relatively new but has already become a serious category with many good preforming funds getting tagged to it. Multicap is a brand new category and has very few funds currently due to allocation restriction but we think it is a good category and should have more funds getting launched in the near future. If you are looking for a Multi Cap Fund in your portfolio, then we suggest you look into all Large

& Mid Cap Category, Flexi Cap & Multi Cap Category for your selection and select the best performing in them.

23. WHAT ARE FOCUSED FUNDS? SHOULD I INVEST IN THEM?

Some sectors and stocks continue to do well, and out-do others be it in a bull rally or a bear fall. Even within each sector, some stocks perform better than others while some continue to fall. This is why some investors prefer to stick to concentrated portfolios, which invest in the best ideas and large allocations give them a fighting chance to generate out-sized returns. A 2% weightage to a stock that goes up by 50% in a year will not markedly impact the portfolio, but if the stock has a weightage of 7% then it will definitely impact the portfolio. There are a quite a few funds in the industry that take a focused approach, rather than choose a plain-vanilla diversified portfolio. These focused funds are a recent found love of Mutual Fund houses and SEBI in 2017 had formalized it with a separate category of Focused Funds where funds cannot keep more than 30 stocks in the portfolio. SEBI has not put any restriction on stock capitalisation, so they can work as pure Flexi Cap Funds.

Many consider concentration in a portfolio as a sign of greater conviction. For a fund manager who is pretty sure that his/her ideas will work, strict diversification can be a problem. This is where a concentrated portfolio of 25-30 stocks can do very well compared to a basket of 50-60 stocks where everybody gets much lower allocation. The reverse situation can play out as well, because concentrated bets can lose a lot of money if the ideas flop. The larger the allocation, bigger would be the losses in an unfortunate case. So clearly, these funds are riskier than your regular Flexi Cap Funds.

This category has relatively older funds such as DSP Focused Fund and Axis Focused 25 Fund which are more tilted towards large caps and IDFC Focused Equity Fund which is focused more towards Mid & Small Caps. And then there are new entrants after SEBI categorization such as Franklin India Focused Equity Fund (a Flexi-Cap Category Fund before), Nippon Focused Equity Fund (a Small & Midcap Category Fund before) & SBI Focused Equity Fund (a Mid Cap Category Fund before) which re-aligned their portfolios based on Focused category mandate.

Overall, this category has seen high growth in AUM and new NFOs due to good performances but it is clearly a riskier category w.r.t to peers such as Flexi Cap & Large Caps due to more concentrated bets and performance could be very different among funds due to different views of Fund Managers. You can take allocation if you are convinced with the Fund Manager's skills.

24. WHAT ARE VALUE & CONTRA FUNDS? HOW ARE THEY DIFFERENT FROM OTHER DIVERSIFIED FUNDS?

Stock Market investing follows two major styles – Growth & Value investing.

Growth stock investing is a style of investing that holds growth stocks, which are stocks of companies that are expected to grow at a rate faster in relation to the overall stock market. The optimism is reflected in the premium valuation commanded by the market price of such companies. Typically, growth stocks have low dividend yields and above-average valuations as measured by price-to-earnings (P/E), market capitalisation-to-sales and price-to-book value ratios (P/B), reflecting the market's high expectations of superior growth. Some of the sectors such as Chemical, Infra & Technology are examples of Growth sectors seen as of Dec 2022. All major funds focus on Growth or blended (Growth+Value) style of investing.

Value stock investing primarily invest in value stocks, which are stocks that an investor believes are selling at a price that is low in relation to earnings or other fundamental value measures. In simple terms, the value investors or fund managers are looking for stocks selling at a "discount;" they want to find a bargain. These investors or managers often employ the fundamental analysis approach to researching and analysing corporations to determine if the stock(s) should be purchased -- to see if it's a "good value." value stocks usually have above-average dividend yields and low P/Es. SEBI had created a separate category of Value Funds which will completely focus on this style of investing. They don't have any restriction in investing though and will work like Flexi Cap Funds. This category has some very good performing funds such as ICICI Prudential Value Discovery Fund, HDFC Capital Builder Value Fund etc.

Then there is a third way of investing which is actually a subset of Value Investing – **Contra Stock Investing**. In contra investing, the fund manager focuses on investing against the prevailing market trend in assets that are performing poorly and selling them when they perform well. The approach is based on identifying neglected stocks that are undervalued today (trading at lower P/E multiple or P/BV), but have a potential of growing in the long-term. Contra investing is far more complex than value investing, as the objective is picking stocks which are dumped by the market (available at a cheap price) in the short-term, but nonetheless have the potential to gain in the long-term when the market recognises its true potential. Hence by doing so, contra investing aims at sailing against the tide by betting on "out of favour" stocks / sectors, in an attempt to gain in the long-term. SBI Contra and Invesco Contra Fund are the two good performing Contra Funds.

Hospitality, PSU Banks and Aviation were considered three sectors which were 'out of favour' in the years 2021 and 2022 (due to Covid) and were being used by Contra or Value investing fund managers.

Our Take: Even though Value & Contra Investing strategy seems very attractive and works on Warren Buffet principles but in high Growth markets such as India, it is equally difficult to implement. Good value opportunities are scarce and when they come, there are many takers. Due to this, value and contra funds too have some allocation to growth stocks.

Value or Contra Funds are for patient investors. These funds mostly under-perform in high growth years which many of the investors may not like. Performance of these funds are also highly dependent on skillset of Fund manager who should be able to distinguish well between bad stock and badly beaten good stock.

25. SIX THINGS TO CONSIDER BEFORE I START EQUITY MF INVESTMENTS?

Equity Mutual Fund investments are risky as compared to Debt Investments as these funds directly invest in the stock market. So, you should consider some important things before investing in equity mutual funds:

1. Can be volatile in short term: Stock market performance is dependent on a lot of factors – Economy, Company's management, Sector performance, Govt. Policy, Global Markets etc. These factors lead to volatility in market returns on a day to day basis. But in long term, returns tend to be stable. So, you should always invest in equity mutual fund for your long-term goals. **Example**, on 26st Jan 23, YTD (year to date) returns of Small Cap Equity Funds were (-)1.85% whereas trailing returns for 10 years were 18.33% p.a.

2. Select Right Fund: There are more than 3000 Fund schemes to choose from. Selecting a right fund before actually

investing is important. It should be analysed based on the fund manager's performance, previous years' returns, fund rating by Fund-o-meter, etc. You should always consult your advisor before finalizing.

3. Fund Cost: The charges levied by a fund must be considered which include Expense ratio, Exit load policies, etc. There are fund schemes with Expense ratio of less than 1% and as high as 3% as well. So, choose your fund wisely.

4. Type of Risk Profile: Different types of Equity Funds have different risk profiles. Small and Mid-Cap funds have very high risk, whereas Large Cap funds have lowest in equity asset class. To mitigate this risk, you should invest in small and mid-cap funds for a longer duration than compared with Large and Flexi cap funds. Sector funds bet on certain sectors, thus they carry highest risk. So, you should pick a fund such that fund's risk profile matches your investment objective.

5. Tax Implication: Domestic Equity Funds enjoy lesser long-term capital gains tax i.e. 10%, compared to short term capital gains tax (15%). So, try NOT to redeem your investments before 1 year.

6. Invest via Systematic way: You should minimize putting lump sum amount in Equity Funds as with lump sum investments you tend to time the market, whereas with SIPs your investments will be averaged across a time period of your investment. We will discuss about them in this book's Category 9 (Systematic Transactions).

CATEGORY 3

Debt Mutual Funds

"You've always got to think about having some fixed income in your portfolio as well as equities."

–Charles Schwab

26. WHAT IS A DEBT MUTUAL FUND?

"Debt" the word itself means loan. Debt mutual fund gives loans to government, businesses and financial institutions and hence Debt funds invest into fixed income securities such as Treasury Bills, Government Securities, Corporate Bonds, Money Market instruments and other debt instruments of different time horizons. Debt Funds attract Short Term Capital Gain tax for investment below 3 years and Long Term Capital Gains Tax for investments above 3 years.

Examples: Aditya Birla SL Short Term Fund, HDFC short term fund, ICICI Prudential Long Term Fund, etc.

27. IN WHAT TYPE OF SECURITIES DOES THE DEBT FUND INVEST?

There are different type of Debt or Fixed Income Securities which Debt Funds invest in. Overall, Fixed Income securities are divided into two portions –

1. Fixed Income Securities Issued by Government – Here are details:

Treasury Bills: Treasury bills (T-bills) are money market instruments, i.e., short-term debt instruments issued by the Government of India, and are issued in three tenures—91 days, 182 days, and 364 days. The T-bills are zero coupon securities and pay no interest. They are issued at a discount and are redeemed at face value on maturity.

Cash Management Bills: Cash management bills (CMBs) have the generic characteristics of T-bills but are issued for a maturity period less than 91 days. Like the T-bills, they are also issued at a discount, and are redeemed at face value on maturity.

Dated Government Securities: Dated government securities are long-term securities that carry a fixed or floating coupon (interest rate), which is paid on the face value, payable at fixed time periods (usually half-yearly). The tenure of dated securities can be up to 30 years.

<u>State Development Loans</u>: State governments also raise loans from the market. State Development Loans (SDLs) are dated securities issued through an auction similar to the auctions conducted for the dated securities issued by the central government. Interest is serviced at half-yearly intervals, and the principal is repaid on the maturity date. Like the dated securities issued by the central government, the SDLs issued by the state governments qualify for SLR (Statutory Liquidity Ratio), that is a portion of deposits has be to maintained in liquid sovereign securities.

2. Fixed Income Securities Issued by Corporates – Here are details:

<u>Certificate of Deposits (CDs)</u>

A Certificate of Deposit (CD) is a money market instrument which is issued in a dematerialised form against funds deposited in a bank for a specific period. Certificates of Deposit are issued by scheduled commercial banks and selected financial institutions in India as allowed by RBI within a limit.

<u>Commercial Papers (CPs)</u>

Commercial paper is an unsecured, short-term debt instrument issued by a corporation, typically for the financing of accounts receivable, inventories and meeting short-term liabilities.

<u>Call/Notice Money</u>

It means a loan for very short period i.e., one to fourteen days. The loans are repayable on demand at the option of either the lender or the borrower. Call money is money at call. Call money market is a market where short-term surplus funds of commercial banks, and other financial institutions, are traded.

The participants, usually, borrow and lend call/ notice money for one day/ for a period up to 14 days. The call money market is the highly liquid market and there is no collateral involved, and accounts for a large share of the total turnover of the money market. Overnight Debt Funds invest their large portfolio in this instrument.

<u>Commercial Bills</u>

Commercial bills arise out of trade transactions. When goods are sold on credit the seller draws a bill on the buyer for the due amount. The buyer accepts it agreeing to pay the amount after specific period to the person mentioned in the bill or to the bearer of the bill. It is drawn for a short period ranging from three to six months.

These bills are transferable by endorsement and delivery and can be discounted or rediscounted. In a bill market the bill of exchanges are bought and sold.

The seller can get payment immediately by discounting the bills with commercial banks or other financial intermediaries. At maturity date the intermediary claims the amount of money from the person who has accepted the Bill.

Very similar concept as Banker's acceptance. Banker's acceptance is majorly used for export import transactions whereas commercial bills is used for other local transactions.

<u>NCDs</u> - Non-convertible debentures (NCDs) are fixed income instruments where you are promised a certain interest for a fixed tenure. It is a type of Corporate debt where companies issue NCDs when they want to raise money for various needs such as expansion. The NCD is a promise that the company will pay back the money at a promised interest rate. It is closed-ended debt instrument, which means it is available for subscription only for a particular period. The main attraction of NCDs was high return

to investors in comparison to other fixed income instruments like bank deposits.

28. SHOULD I INVEST IN DEBT MUTUAL FUNDS?

Debt Funds Pros and Cons

Debt Funds are an excellent alternative to other deposit schemes such as Bank deposits or Post Office deposits or other govt. small saving schemes. Let's discuss their pros and cons:

Advantages of Debt Mutual Funds

<u>No Lock in</u>: An open-ended debt fund is very liquid so one can withdraw money as and when one requires. There is no lock in.

<u>Better Returns</u>: Few types of Debt Funds have given few percentage point better returns than other popular deposit schemes.

<u>Less Risky</u>: Debt Funds are not dependent on stock market changes and hence are significantly less volatile and less risky than Equity Funds.

<u>Tax Deferred</u>: Taxation of Debt Funds is applicable only when they are redeemed or switched. You don't need to pay taxation on accrual basis like in FDs. More details in *Q33*.

<u>Diversification</u>: Each debt fund invests in number of fixed income securities and hence hedges the risk of default.

<u>Access to Institutional Securities</u>: Debt funds bring you the securities in which retail investors cannot invest directly.

Disadvantages of Debt Mutual Funds

<u>Interest Rate Risk</u>: Debt Funds carry interest rate risk and can add/reduce your capital based on interest rate movement.

<u>No Control</u>: Investors don't have any control over investments, as fund manager manages them.

<u>Credit Risk</u>: Some Debt fund manager take credit risk to get higher returns by buying bonds of small companies, which give higher interest rate but have higher chances of default.

<u>High Expense Ratio</u>: Some debt funds have expense ratio of as high as 2.1% which is deducted from your total return. This expense ratios could be a high percentage of your yearly returns.

Our Take:

Debt mutual funds are suitable for your short-term goals (<3 years) or for investors who are conservative, not active in the market and require regular income. The debt mutual funds can provide regular income and are less risky and you should have lower return expectations from them. When your long-term goals come within 3 years range for which you have been investing into equity, you should shift your corpus into debt funds to keep it secure and still growing till the time you actually reach your goal.

29. WHAT ARE VARIOUS TYPES OF DEBT FUNDS?

There are different types of Debt Mutual Funds that invest in various fixed income securities of different time horizons. SEBI has defined these types based on Macaulay's Duration of the fund. Below is the classification of debt funds based on SEBI notification 'Categorization & Rationalization of Mutual Fund Schemes' dated October 6th, 2017. Please remember return expectation in the table below is assuming you will hold the fund for full investment horizon.

Type of Debt Fund	Investment Horizon (Duration)	Investment In	Pre-Tax Returns Expectation (p.a.)	Points to Note
Overnight Fund	1 Day	Call Money Market	New Category. Should be 4-5%	Safest & most Liquid, No Exit Load. Should be compared to Savings Banks returns.

Liquid/ Money Market Funds	1-90 days	Treasury bills (short term Govt. securities)	4-6%	Highly Liquid, No Exit Load. Should be compared to Savings Banks account returns.
Ultra-Short Duration Funds	3-6 months	Treasury Bills, Commercial Papers	5-7%	Also, known as Liquid Plus Funds, No Exit Load
Low Duration Fund	6-12 months	Treasury Bills, Commercial Papers & Commercial Deposits	5-7%	Mostly No Exit Load
Money Market Fund	0 – 12 Months	Any Money Market Instrument – CP, CD, T-Bill, CBLO etc	5-7%	Mostly No Exit Load
Short Duration Funds	1 Year – 3 Years	Corporate Bonds & Debentures	6-7.5%	Lower risk, may have small (0.25-0.5%) exit load for max a month
Medium Duration Funds	3 years – 4 Years	Corporate Bonds, Debentures and Govt. Securities	5-7.5%	Medium Risk, should be compared to 3yrs Bank FDs
Medium to Long Duration Fund	4 Years – 7 Years	Corporate Bonds, Debentures and Govt. Securities	5-7.5%	Medium to High Risk, should be compared to 5 yrs Bank FDs
Long Duration Funds	7+ Years	Corporate Bonds, Debentures and Govt. Securities	6-8 %	Highest Risk Debt Funds. Mostly gave very low returns in last 1 year due to increasing interest rates (as of 25th May 2022)

Dynamic Bond Funds	Not fixed. Depends on Fund Manager's view of interest rate changes	All Debt Instruments	7-9%	Medium-High Risk, can shift between maturities aggressively
Corporate Bond Fund	Not fixed. Mostly similar to Short/ Medium Duration	Highest Rated Corporate Bonds – Min 80% Asset	6–8%	Medium Interest Rate Risk
Credit Risk Funds	Similar to Short/ Medium Duration	Low Rated and high yield Corporate Bonds – Min 65% Assets	3-9%	Low-Medium Interest Rate risk but High Credit Risk
Banking & PSU Funds	Similar to Short/ Medium Duration	Debt instruments of banks, PSUs, Public Financial Institutions - 80% of total assets	7.5–8.5%	Similar profile as Corporate Bond Funds but with better credit rating
Gilt Funds	Mostly > 3 years	Govt. securities – Min 80%	5-9%	High Interest Rate Risk due to large maturities, zero credit risk as Govt. will never default
Gilt Fund with 10 year constant duration	10 Years	Govt. securities – Min 80%	5-9%	High Interest Rate Risk due to large maturities, zero credit risk as Govt. will never default

Floater Funds	Mostly similar to Short/ Medium Duration	Floating Rate Instruments – Min 65%	6.5-8%	Floating Rate Instruments are those whose interest rate changes with the market condition

Following chart gives these classifications by Risk levels for better understanding:

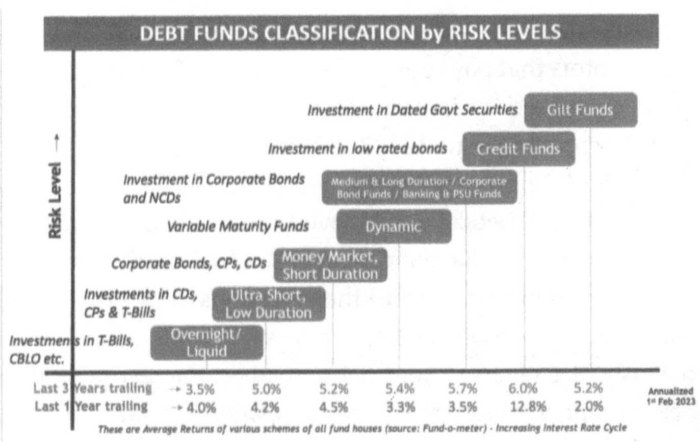

30. HOW DEBT FUNDS WORK?

Debt mutual funds are mutual funds that invest in fixed income instruments. Just like Equity market, there is a bond market where all the fixed income securities in which Debt Funds invest, can be traded. Debt mutual funds are like baskets that hold dozens or hundreds of individual securities (like, corporate bonds, govt. securities etc.). A Debt fund manager researches fixed income markets for the best bonds based upon the overall objective of the fund. The manager then purchases and sells bonds based upon economic and market activity. And then, this interest income that the fund receives from the bonds they invest in, is passed on to you.

Why bond prices rise and fall? Majorly due to change or expectation of change in interest rate.

Now, what is a bond? It is a promised interest rate for a fixed duration of a security. So, when the interest rate falls in the market, demand for these high interest rate bonds increases. And when the interest rate increases in the market, interest rates promised for these bonds would not seem attractive and hence, demand for such bonds would fall.

Let's understand this with an **example**: Suppose there's a bond of Tata Motors that pays out interest at a rate of 9% per annum. But RBI decreased the interest rates in the economy and newer bonds start getting issued at 8%. Obviously, the old bond would now be worth more than earlier and if there is an expectation of more rate cut, people would love to buy old bonds. Its price would now rise in the bond market. Mutual funds that hold Tata Motors bond would find their holdings worth more and they could make additional profits by selling this bond. Again, obviously, the reverse could happen when interest rates rise. Therefore, Bond prices hold inverse relationship with Interest rates.

Now important thing to note here is that price doesn't change only when RBI changes interest rates but it changes on a daily basis, why? Because of the change of expectation based on number of internal & external factors – Inflation figures, Economic Growth figures, Global Liquidity etc.

In FY 2022-23, Interest rates were seen going up due to high inflation in India & globe due to which all long term debt funds gave very low return and short duration funds gave better returns and some of the Gilt Funds actually gave negative returns. Check Q29 chart which helps you understand the difference in returns of last 1 year and 3 year (Trailing returns)

31. ARE DEBT FUNDS REALLY SAFE?

No doubt that Debt Funds are safer/less risky than Equity products as they do not invest in any stock market instrument. But we should know that Debt Funds are not completely risk free either, they inherently carry 2 major types of risks and each Debt Fund type has them in different degrees:

a. <u>Interest Rate Risk</u>: Bond prices generally rise or fall in response to interest rate changes, or like any market, the expectation of interest rate changes. Higher the maturity period of the bond, more sensitive they are to change in interest rate. During the falling interest rate period, the debt fund's yield improves, and they give better returns and vice-versa during increasing interest rate period. This risk is maximum in Gilt Funds as their average maturity period is very high (10+ years) and least in overnight & liquid funds which have maturity of not more than 90 days. This risk can be minimized by opting for short term maturity funds or by matching your period of investment with what is called the 'maturity' of the debt funds, which can also be achieved by investing in Closed Ended FMPs.

b. <u>Credit Risk</u>: Second risk is the risk of default by the company whose security is bought by the debt fund manager. Companies which are not much known or are new, mostly issue their bonds at higher interest rates than established players to attract investments but they carry credit risk as well. This risk is highest in Credit Risk Funds as they take credit risk to earn higher return than other debt funds. Credit Risk was the major risk that weighed in closing of 6 debt schemes by Franklin Templeton (Discussed in detail in Q40). You can minimize this risk by investing in Debt funds such as Gilt Funds, which carry zero Credit risk as all the investment is done in Govt. Securities or in Corporate Bond funds which only invest in highest rated bonds (AAA or AA), where risk of default is minimum.

Apart from above two risks, Debt funds do carry liquidity risk (low volume trade of certain securities) and Inflation risk like any other debt instrument.

32. DIFFERENCE BETWEEN DEBT FUNDS AND BANK FIXED DEPOSIT?

This is one of the most frequently asked questions. The love for fixed deposits (FD) among Indians is second to none. The strong association with FDs, however, can be attributed to the fact that they are easy to understand and execute, offer reasonably good interest rates, are relatively safe and, provide guaranteed return at maturity. But are Bank FDs better than Debt Mutual Funds? Let's find out:

Basis	Debt Funds	Fixed Deposits
Working	With your investments, Debt Funds buy Corporate bonds, debentures or Govt. securities. Basically, give loans to Corporates or Government.	With your investments, Banks give loans to individuals or corporates.
Risk	Low to Medium depending on type. Short Term Funds carry low risk whereas Credit Risk or Gilt Funds carry medium to High risk.	Very low to low risk as Banks rarely default and Govt. also gives guarantee on first ₹5 Lakh of your deposits.
Returns	Based on market movement. 3-7% (after deducting expense ratio) returns have been given in last 1-3 years based on the type of Fund. The returns are highly dependent on interest rate scenario.	Currently between 5.0-6.5% based on maturity and bank (as of 1st Feb 2023).

Liquidity	Very Liquid. You can redeem your investments anytime.	Liquid if premature withdrawal is allowed. Also, loan against Bank FDs are easily available.
Premature withdrawal	There is an Exit load on few of the schemes if withdrawal is done before a stipulated period. Many schemes with zero exit load or lesser duration soft lock are available too. But if the investments are withdrawn within 3 years, the returns are taxed as per your tax slab.	Possible with penalty between 1-1.5%
Taxation	From 1st April, 2023, Debt funds are taxed as per your tax slab. Same as FDs. If you have invested in Debt Funds before 1st April 2023, then you will get Indexation benefit on your taxation. More details in *Q33*.	Returns are taxable as per your tax slab.
Tax Exemption	No Tax Exemption on investment amount.	5 years tax saving FDs get exemption under Section 80 C. But returns are taxed according to your tax slab.
Tax Payment	Another advantage is that you must pay tax only at redemption. So your tax gets deferred.	You must pay tax on accrued interest earned each year irrespective of whether you have redeemed your investments or not.
TDS	No for Resident Indians. Yes, for NRIs. Same tax applicable for as residents.	Yes, if the interest earned is more than ₹40,000/- year a TDS at 10% is levied if the PAN is provided and if it is not provided, 20% tax is levied for domestic deposits. In case of NRO deposits, a TDS of 31.2% is applicable. Additional surcharge is applicable for interest income above Rs. 50 Lacs

Options	Too many options to choose from with different investment types, maturities and risks.	Standard product offered by each bank.

Our Take:

Debt Funds score a bit over Fixed deposits because of liquidity, better returns and lesser paperwork due to no TDS, but then you need to be careful while choosing the right fund for you in the sea of the options available and each have different risk profile. Your choice should match with your return and holding period expectations.

33. HOW ARE DEBT FUNDS RETURNS TAXED?

Taxation for Investments done on or after 1st April 2023

There was a major change in Debt Fund taxation from 1st April 2023. All Debt Funds bought on or after 1st April, 2023 will have taxation at par with Fixed Deposits. It means all the gains from debt funds will be added to your income of the year of redemption and taxed as per applicable tax slab. Like earlier, there will be no benefit of Long Term Capital Gain Tax on Debt Funds on investment done on or after 1st April, 2023.

Same Taxation is applicable on FoFs, International Funds and Gold/Silver Funds too. So above changes from 1st April 2023 are applicable on these categories of the funds too.

Example: If your gains (short term or long term, doesn't matter) from Debt Funds (invested on or after 1st April 2023) are ₹50,000 on day of redemption and your tax slab is 30%, then you will have to pay ₹15000 tax on gains as per new rule irrespective of holding period.

Taxation for Investments done before 1st April 2023

However, if you have invested in Debt Funds or Intl' Funds, FoFs, Gold or Silver Fundsbefore 1st April 2023, then the taxation of capital gains on those funds will be like earlier which is mentioned in table below -

	Holding Period	**Taxation**
Short Term Capital Gain	Less than 36 months	Gains added to your income of the year of redemption and taxed as per applicable tax slab
Long Term Capital Gain	More than 36 months	You will have to pay 20% tax on gains after Indexation

Indexation means adjustment of gains with respect to Inflation i.e. subtracting the impact of inflation on your returns and then paying taxes. Inflation here is calculated based on CII (Cost Inflation Index) provided by Income tax department each year. Let us understand the calculations with an **example**:

Suppose you invested ₹10 lakhs in 2010-2011 in a Debt Fund. Assuming the fund returned 10 percent a year, and you redeem it for ₹16,10,510 after 5 years i.e. in 2015-16. Since you sold the fund after 36 months of holding period, your capital gains will be considered as Long term Capital gains. Capital gains in this example would be ₹6,10,510 (Redemption amount – Invested Amount).

Now CII (available on Income Tax Dept. website) for 2010-11 was 167 and 2015-16 was 254. So, we will adjust the value of our investments made in 2010-11 to the value of the same investments which stand as of 2015-16 i.e. year of redemption. The calculation is done as follows:

(CII at redemption Year/CII at Investment Year) X Invested amount = Indexed Investment amount

254/167*10 Lakh = ₹15,20,958 (Indexed Investment Amount)

So, now the long-term capital gain would be

Redemption amount - Indexed Investment amount = ₹16,10,510 – ₹ 15,20,958 = ₹89,552

A 20% taxation on this amount would be ₹17,910. This is less than 3% of your gains (₹6,10,510). Hence, we will be paying taxes on the returns earned over and above the inflation adjusted initial investment.

<u>Taxation on Dividends</u>

Any dividend declared by mutual fund houses (in Dividend or Dividend Re-investment Plan) is added to your income and is taxed as per your tax slab. DDT was removed in Budget 2021. Earlier, DDT (Dividend Distribution Tax) was deducted by Mutual Fund houses and the dividends were tax free in the hands of investors.

<u>Similar Taxation is applicable on FoFs, International Funds and Gold/Silver Funds too.</u>

34. WHAT ARE GILT FUNDS? SHOULD I INVEST?

Basis	Description
Description	Gilt funds are a type of mutual funds, which invest exclusively in government securities. Hence these funds are choice of investors who are very conservative and who can take very low risk. "Government security (G-Sec)" means a security created and issued by the Government for raising a public loan or for any other purpose as may be notified by the Government in the Official Gazette. While these can be short-term securities, a good number are long-term gilts. The G-Sec market is largely dominated by institutional investors and gilt funds are an easy avenue for retail investors to participate in the market.
Investment made in	Only Govt. Securities.
Liquidity	They are one of the most liquid debt funds as secondary market of Govt. securities is active and has good volumes. Most of the debt funds do not charge any Exit load on such funds.
Risk	Highly sensitive to Interest rate changes as they have very large maturities. Among Debt funds, they have the highest interest rate risk but almost no Credit or Default risk. Since they only invest in Govt. securities which are sovereign rated, there is no risk of default.

Returns	They give low returns in increasing interest rate cycle and vice-versa. Like in the current increasing interest rate cycle, as on 1st Feb 2023, this category on average has given 2.5% in last one year and 5.46% p.a. in last 3 years. Generally high interest rate cycle is followed by a decreasing rate spell and so mostly starting latter half of 2023, gilt fund should be seen giving good returns in the short term.
Example	SBI Magnum Gilt Fund, is the biggest Debt Fund by Asset under management in this category.

Our Take:

You should invest in long term Gilt Funds only when the inflation and interest rates have peaked. If you do not know about it, do not invest!

35. WHAT ARE CREDIT RISK FUNDS? HOW RISKY ARE THEY?

Basis	Description
Definition	Credit Risk funds (Earlier Called as Credit Opportunities Funds) take credit risk for the sake of generating high yield. For this, they adopt the accrual strategy to provide a better return. Accrual strategy is nothing but buying a company with lower credit ratings at the moment, hoping that the ratings go up. Here, the Fund manager adds a lower-rated paper in the hopes of generating higher returns as mostly low-rated papers give higher returns to attract buyers and if their ratings improve in future, their value increases even more.
Investment made in	65-100% of the assets are invested in low credit rated (Below AA) debt instruments. It is compulsory for all Debt instruments to get a credit rating from leading agencies such as ICRA, CARE & CRISIL
Risk	They have low to medium interest rate risk but High Credit risk. In the past default or lowering of credit rating has impacted these debt funds returns. Example – Lowering of credit rating of JSPL bonds in 2017, DHFL in 2018 reduced the returns of some of the funds by up to 2%. These funds can also face liquidity risk as the debt instruments they invest in are not very popular and they may face issues while selling them esp. if their credit rating has downgraded.

Returns	These type of funds typically give better returns than similar maturity debt funds. But last few years (2018-2021) have been very bad in terms of returns due to multiple defaults like IL&FS, DHFL etc. Returns of these funds are also highly dependent on Fund Manager skills as they have to conduct their own due diligence and choose the right assets which even though may have low credit rating but a bright future.
Example *(Data as on 1st Feb 2023)*	HDFC Credit Risk Fund is one of the popular Credit Risk Funds which has almost 55% of total assets in AA or Below rated papers

Our Take: Credit Risk Funds are one of the riskiest debt funds. Due to their high credit risk, they are highly dependent on Fund Manager skills. They are for high risk investors who want to invest money for short term in Debt market (less than 3 years). Investors who seek a steady income and want to keep the risk factor minimal should stay away from this category of funds.

36. DIFFERENCE BETWEEN FLOATER DEBT AND DYNAMIC DEBT FUNDS?

Factors	Floater Debt Funds	Dynamic Debt Funds
Product	These funds invest majority of their assets in Floating Rate securities i.e. securities whose coupon rate changes as the benchmark interest rate change. It is not as simple as it appear as there aren't many issuers of floating rate bonds (esp. in low interest rate scenarios). Thus, these funds employ a derivative strategy to comply with the minimum 65% investment in floating rate bonds by using a combination of fixed rate bonds and Interest Rate Swaps.	As the name suggests, these funds have flexibility to invest in all kind of fixed income instruments based on the Fund Manager's view of interest rate cycle. So, if interest rates are expected to grow, they would invest in short term instruments and vice-versa.

Risk	These are very low to low risk products as they are mostly immune to interest rate risks.	These are medium to high risk and their performance and returns are highly dependent on Fund Manager's market reading and forecast.
Returns	These give above average returns in increasing interest rate scenario and average in falling interest rate market.	These can give very good returns in both increasing and falling interest rate scenarios but it heavily depends on the Fund Manager. Funds gave lower than other category returns in 2017 & 2022 as many fund manager predicted the wrong interest rate cycle.
Recommendation	These are an excellent emergency fund as these carry very low risk and have no exit load.	These are all-season funds and can give above average returns in all market conditions, given that the Fund Manager is an expert.
Random Example (Data as on 1st Feb 2023)	Aditya Birla Sunlife Floating Rate Fund - Direct Expense: 0.23% Last 3-year return: 5.81% p.a. Last one year return: 5.15% Exit Load: 0%	Aditya Birla Sunlife Dynamic Bond Fund - Direct Expense: 0.58% Last 3-year return: 7.32% p.a. Last one year return: 7.01% Exit Load: 0.5% on 85% of corpus for 90 days

37. CORPORATE BONDS VS CORPORATE FDS VS DEBT MUTUAL FUND?

Basis	Corporate Bonds	Corporate FDs	Debt Funds
Definition	Corporate bonds are debt securities issued by private and public corporations. When one buys a corporate bond, one lends money to the	The deposit placed by investors with companies for a fixed term carrying a prescribed rate of interest is called Company Fixed	Debt Funds are a basket of debt securities and invest in bonds, company FDs, government securities and

	issuing company. In exchange, the company promises to return the money on a specified maturity date. Until that date, the company usually pays you a stated rate of interest, generally semi-annually.	Deposit. Deposits thus mobilized are governed by the Companies Act.	other debt instruments.
Safety	They are secured debt instruments as they are backed by assets, which depositors can claim if the company fails to repay. They are still highly risky as investor is dependent on company's performance and if it defaults, mostly investor don't get much.	They are unsecured and not backed by assets. Riskier than Corporate Bond.	They hedge their risk by investing in mix of Govt. securities, corporate bonds and other deposits. Are mostly safest among three.
Liquidity	Tradable on exchange and hence can be sold anytime but liquidity is a concern and you may not always find a buyer.	Not tradable on exchange. Premature withdrawals are allowed with interest rate penalty.	Since debt funds invest in many debt instruments of different maturities, investments in debt funds are very liquid. Many do charge some exit load if redemption is done before a stipulated period.
Returns	Their returns are impacted by interest rate changes and you can earn or lose money on coupon rate if you withdraw prematurely.	Here returns are fixed just like bank deposits. No impact of interest rate changes. Interest depends on type of	Depending on the type of Debt fund, they are also impacted by interest rate changes. Returns depend

		company. Established players offer low interest rates.	on type of debt fund and movement of interest rate cycle.
	Depending on type of security, they mostly give higher interest rates than debt funds.		
Credit Rating	It is mandatory for issuers to get the instrument rated by at least one rating agency such as CRISIL or ICRA.	It is mandatory for NBFC deposits but not for other corporates.	Most of the Debt funds invest majority of their money in high rated debt instruments only, to decrease their risk. It is important to check overall Risk profile of the fund.
Taxation	Returns are taxed as per your tax slab unless these are Tax Free Bonds (issued by few sectors which Govt. wants to promote). If you sell your bonds on an exchange prior to maturity, capital gain tax would apply.	Taxed as per your tax slab	Taxed as per your tax slab. Discussed in detail in Q33.
TDS	Bonds in demat form have no TDS applicable	10% TDS is applicable if interest exceeds ₹5000 in a financial year	No TDS

Our Take:

Unless, you are a very hands-on investor and do detailed analysis before investing, you should always invest in debt securities through Debt Fund mode. As it not only gives you diversification benefit but also gives you access to the expertise of a fund manager and his/her team. It also gives better liquidity.

38. HOW CREDIT RATING IN DEBT MUTUAL FUNDS WORK?

Each bond issued in India has to compulsory take Credit Rating from any major Rating agency like Crisil (S&P), Care, IndiaRating, Fitch, ICRA(Moody). Bonds issued by Government automatically gets SOV rating and is the highest safety rating. Based on the company's performance who is issuing the bond, these rating agencies give credit rating based on following nomenclature:

Credit Rating Scales by Agency, Long-Term

Moody's	S&P	Fitch		
Aaa	AAA	AAA	Prime	
Aa1	AA+	AA+	High grade	
Aa2	AA	AA		
Aa3	AA-	AA-		
A1	A+	A+	Upper medium grade	
A2	A	A		
A3	A-	A-		
Baa1	BBB+	BBB+	Lower medium grade	
Baa2	BBB	BBB		
Baa3	BBB-	BBB-		
Ba1	BB+	BB+	Non-investment grade speculative	"Junk"
Ba2	BB	BB		
Ba3	BB-	BB-		
B1	B+	B+	Highly speculative	
B2	B	B		
B3	B-	B-		
Caa1	CCC+	CCC	Substantial risk	
Caa2	CCC		Extremely speculative	
Caa3	CCC-		Default imminent with	
Ca	CC	CC	little prospect for	
	C	C	recovery	
C				
/	D	D	In default	
/				

WOLFSTREET.com

These ratings can be upgraded or downgraded too based on company's performance. Debt Mutual Funds give details of ratings of each bond they have in their portfolio every month. These details gives us a good pointer on how much credit risk the debt fund is taking. SOV & AAA are Prime grade bond papers and have lowest risk and hence funds investing primarily in these papers have very low Credit risk. **Example**: Gilt Funds only invest in SOV rated papers and Corporate Bond category primarily invest in AAA rated papers.

39. WHAT ARE SEGREGATED PORTFOLIOS (SIDE POCKETING)? PROVISIONING IN CASE OF DEBT DEFAULTS.

In the year 2018, after NBFC crisis, lot of default started happening. Lot of rating downgrades were done in 2018. Because of these downgrades or these credit events, a lot of debt funds had gone down on their NAV's particularly. This has never been seen before. Earlier it could be seen that these debt funds (esp. credit risk category) would keep growing slowly and continuously and people were comparing these debt funds with fixed deposits but things changed in 2018 and investors realized the risk associated with Debt Funds.

In case of defaults & major rating downgrades, there is a provisioning called segregated portfolio. The concept of a Segregated Portfolio is promoted by the Securities and Exchange Board of India (SEBI) in December 2018 by a circular and is a procedure that allows mutual funds to separate a certain number of units against downgraded debts and money market instruments held by them. To quote from circular - SEBI has decided «to permit creation of segregated portfolio of unrated debt or money market instruments by mutual fund schemes of an issuer that does not have any outstanding rated debt or money market instruments». This is allowed provided that segregated portfolio of such unrated debt or money market instruments may be created only in case of actual default of either the interest or principal amount.

Segregated portfolios is a mechanism to separate illiquid and hard-to-value assets from other more liquid assets in a portfolio. It prevents the distressed assets from damaging the returns generated from more liquid and better-performing assets.

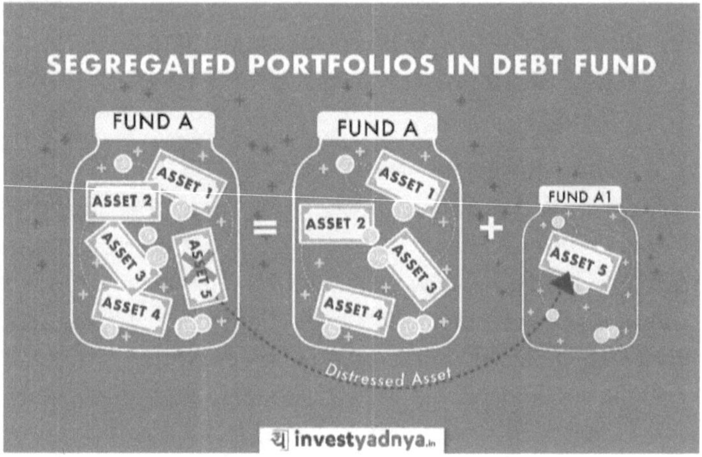

How segregation (Side Pocketing) works in Debt Funds?

It works in the following way:

If a fund has a NAV of Rs 20, of which Rs 2 was invested in a security of a company which has defaulted or its rating has been downgraded, etc, then the fund house can resort to creating a side pocket containing the bad bonds. In such a case, the NAV of the main fund takes a hit and reduces by the amount side pocketed. A new fund is created out of the amount which has been segregated. This new fund has the same number of units as the main fund.

There's a possibility that this money will be recovered. By segregating the bad bonds, investors' interest stays protected because if the bad debt recovers, investors would be the beneficiary. Further, one can redeem and walk out with the remaining money from the main fund.

This side-pocketing provision ensures that the rightful owner remains entitled to the benefits of the recovery in a fund and gets it in the future, subject to realisation.

The total portfolio is the portfolio which is the original one and then is split into two portfolios-main portfolios and segregated portfolios. The main portfolio is the portfolio which is separated from the 'total portfolio' with good debts and can be redeemed by the investor at any point of time. The segregated portfolio is that part of the total portfolio which contains the bad, downgraded and illiquid debts. Unitholders in the scheme are allotted units of the side-pocket, in the same ratio as the investment in the parent scheme.

Units of the side-pocket are not redeemable, while the units in the main/original scheme portfolio are redeemable as usual. In segregated portfolio no fresh subscriptions are allowed. Investors can redeem these units once the money is recovered from the bad debt by the mutual fund scheme.

Example – Nippon India Ultrashort Fund has a segregated portfolio for Altico Capital India Limited.

40. FRANKLIN CLOSED 6 DEBT FUNDS. WHY?

On April 23rd, 2020 the Trustee of Franklin Templeton Mutual Fund decided to wind up six debt schemes.

1. Franklin India Ultra Short Bond Fund
2. Franklin India Short Term Income Fund
3. Franklin India Credit Risk Fund

4. Franklin India Low Duration Fund

5. Franklin India Dynamic Accrual Fund

6. Franklin India Income Opportunities Fund

Winding up means these funds will cease to exist after all the holding they have been sold-off, as and when that happens. And till that time it happens, there will be no purchase (including SIP instalments, Switches & STP) or Redemption or SWP instalments will be allowed from these funds.

As per a report from B&K Securities, the corpus of the six exposed FT funds stood at Rs 47,658 crore at the end of August 2018. It was also the time when liquidity crisis in the shadow banking space began to surface after the first default by IL&FS. Since then, these six closed funds from Franklin Templeton lost a total corpus of Rs 16,804 crore till March 2020. As a result, in a span of 19 months, the reduced corpus stood at Rs 30,854, including Rs 2,753 of borrowing to manage redemption pressure. Worst was yet to come as in April, these funds lost a corpus of Rs 4,075 crore in first 20 days of the month and reduced corpus stood at Rs 26,779 crore on April 20, 2020. This means these debt funds were yet to come out of liquidity drought started in the wake of the shadow banking crisis when COVID-19 blew the knockout punch.

If we look at the list of funds mentioned above, it has all kinds of debt funds, including low duration and ultra-low duration. Now, while all AMCs take risks in funds like Credit Risk Funds to generate high returns, it is only Franklin that decided to follow this strategy even in short duration funds (low and ultra-low duration). Franklin Templeton followed the approach of taking credit risk i.e., investing in low-rated bonds across debt funds with an aim to generate high returns.

Low-rated bonds give a higher interest rate because they carry a higher risk of default, i.e., the borrower not paying back the interest or principal amount. So to compensate for this risk that the Fund Manager takes by investing in these bonds, they tend to give a higher interest rate. This risk of default is called credit risk. The main challenge in these funds is low liquidity in secondary market. So most of these funds were kept till maturity. But these funds have been in existence for many years and have delivered some excellent returns, what went wrong? Well, one word, COVID-19.

COVID-19 + Slow Inflows + Redemption Pressure + Low Liquidity of the Debt papers: A tricky situation

While we are all aware of how stock markets had tumbled amid the COVID-19 crisis, there has also been an equal impact on the bond market (where bonds are traded). Now, as a result of a flight to safety caused by this pandemic, the bond market has become illiquid. What that means is that there are not enough buyers for the bonds, especially of low-rated bonds. Even if there are, they are asking for a considerable discount on the price.

On the other hand, these funds per AMC have seen more than normal redemption pressure as most investors are in need of cash or are liquidating from these funds first than any other debt funds of other AMCs. This is due to previous issues with the debt funds of Franklin Templeton, like the side pocketing, voluntary markdowns that saw steep fall in returns, etc in 2018-19. What compounded the problem was the inflows in the funds had also slowed down substantially due to the previous issues we just described.

Now, in a normal scenario, a fund will honor these redemption requests by either selling the bonds or borrowing money from banks to pay in case the manager doesn't want to sell at the price he is getting. These funds also resorted to borrowing money, and over the last 6 months, they have been able to manage redemption demand by selling bonds at the right price.

But an ever-increasing redemption pressure, lack of demand for low-rated bonds, and inflows slowing down meant they would have had to sell these bonds at a discount resulting in a loss for investors who were staying invested in these funds. So, technically, the investors who were redeeming were not just creating losses for themselves, but also forcing the Fund Manager to sell at not-so-right-price indirectly hurting other investors in these Funds.

So, best option which Franklin saw in that situation was closing these 6 debt funds completely and give money back whenever they get the money from the debt paper companies. This resulted in many court cases against them and many investor's years of savings stuck with them and finally Supreme Court allowed them to start distributing the cash they have to the investors. This distribution responsibility was given to SBI Mutual Fund by the Supreme Court. Investors started getting their money back now and this was the latest as on 30th Dec 2022 –

Scheme	Total Distribution post payout on December 30, 2022(as a % to April 23, 2020 AUM)[^]	Cash distributed plus AUM of six schemes as on December 30, 2022 (as a % of April 23, 2020 AUM)[^]
Franklin India Ultra Short Bond Fund	108.50%	108.50%
Franklin India Low Duration Fund	112.46%	112.46%
Franklin India Short Term Income Plan	98.20%	106.91%
Franklin India Income Opportunities Fund	108.18%	108.18%
Franklin India Credit Risk Fund	108.59%	113.20%
Franklin India Dynamic Accrual Fund	107.15%	107.15%
Total	106.46%	108.99%

Source: https://www.franklintempletonindia.com

CATEGORY 4

Liquid Mutual Funds

41. WHAT IS A LIQUID CATEGORY FUND?

Liquid Category Fund are debt mutual funds, which invests into fixed income instruments of very short term like commercial papers, treasury bills, certificate of deposits, CBLO etc. with maturity of upto 180 days. Though formally there is no separate category by this name and is actually part of Debt Funds only, we have separated it out as they have some key differences. As per latest categorization of Funds by SEBI, Liquid category has three different types –

1. Overnight Fund – Most liquid fund which can invest in only debt papers with max 1-day maturity. They mostly invest in CBLO or Call Money Market. These funds will have almost negligible Interest rate & Credit risk.

2. Liquid Fund – These types of funds can invest in debt papers with max 91 days maturity. They mostly invest in 91-Day T-Bills and short term CPs & CDs. They have almost negligible credit risk and very low interest rate risk.

3. Ultra-Short Duration Fund (Earlier known as Liquid Plus) – These types of funds can invest in debt papers with max 180 days maturity. They mostly invest in short term CPs & CDs

All these funds are available in growth and dividend options. Dividends can be on daily, weekly, monthly or quarterly basis. Other important features of these funds:

a. They do not charge any exit load and hence are very liquid

b. They also do not have any fixed return rate and returns depend on current market conditions

c. They are the safest Debt Funds type

d. They have the lowest expense ratio among debt funds

e. Ideal for parking your emergency funds or corpus for short time

f. Their returns should be compared with your Savings Bank return

g. Money gets credited with 1-2 working day in your bank account after your redeem it.

h. Out of above 3 types, currently Liquid Funds of many fund house (like ICICI, SBI, Axis, Nippon, ABSL, Kotak, DSP) offer instant redemption facility. Under this facility, you can redeem upto Rs 50,000 per day (or 90% of your Fund value, whichever is lower), instantly in your savings account (within minutes, even if it is a holiday on that day). This facility, in all likelihood will be extended to Overnight Funds as well.

Example: SBI Liquid Fund, HDFC Overnight Fund, ICICI Prudential Ultra Short Term Fund etc.

42. LIQUID FUNDS VS SAVINGS BANK ACCOUNT

Factors	Savings Account	Liquid Fund
Product	Savings account is a deposit account offered by a bank or post office, which provides security of the principal amount and pays interest on it.	It is a debt mutual fund, which invests into fixed income instruments of very short term maturities (a day to 180 days) like commercial papers, treasury bills, certificate of deposits, etc.
Risk	Almost No Risk	Very Low as these funds invest in instruments which are Sovereign Rated Government treasury bills, high credit rated Certificate of Deposits and Commercial Papers. Also, these instruments are not traded in the market and are kept till maturity. So, there is no short-term interest rate risk as well.

Returns	Fixed interest rate. Normally 3-4% p.a. Some banks may offer slightly higher rates but ask for higher amount of deposits. IDFC First Bank gives 6.00% if balance in account is less than ₹1 Lakh (as of 27th Jan 2023).	In the last year, on average liquid funds have given returns in the range of 3-5%.
Taxes	If the interest earned in a year exceeds ₹10,000, the interest is added to your gross income and taxed as per tax slab.	Taxes on returns of these funds are same as other debt funds, as discussed in *Q33*.
Liquidity	You can take out your cash anytime through ATM	Once you redeem your investments, it takes minimum 1 working day for the funds to reach your registered bank account. Nowadays, new instant redemption facility is also given by many of fund houses on their liquid funds, through which you can get your money redeemed instantly as well.
Recommendation of Use	Storage of cash required for monthly expense	Your emergency fund could be stored here. In case of sudden inflows, you could put your inflows in liquid funds till you decide where to invest it.
Example	Most of the banks are currently giving 2.90-4% p.a.	HDFC Liquid Fund - Direct (As on 1st Feb, 2023) Expense: 0.20% Last one year return: 4.33% Type: Open-Ended Fund

CATEGORY 5

Hybrid Funds

"Extremes are easy, strive for Balance"

–Colin Wright

43. DO ANY MUTUAL FUNDS INVEST IN BOTH STOCKS AND BONDS?

What are Hybrid Funds?

Yes, these are called Hybrid Funds. These funds combine stocks, bonds & even other assets such as Gold to help investors leverage the high returns from equities while also benefitting from the steadier, but lower returns from debt. These are suitable funds for Moderate Risk takers. Lately, these funds have become very popular due to their good returns and automatic rebalancing of portfolio.

How rebalancing happens? Suppose an Aggressive hybrid fund manager has planned to keep the Equity share at 70% and rest as debt, then if the stock market takes a plunge and Equity share decreases to 60%, then fund manager will buy more stocks when market is low to keep the equity share at 70%. Similarly, if the market gains and equity share increases to 80%, fund manager will sell Equity when the market is high, to buy Debt and maintain the allocation. So, this helps in auto-rebalancing and selling when the markets are high and buying more when markets are low.

Example of Equity Oriented Hybrid Fund:

Franklin India Equity Hybrid Fund: An Aggressive Hybrid Fund started in 1999, with Asset Allocation (as of Feb 2023)- Debt: 27.59%, Equity: 70.04%, Cash: 2.37%

44. HOW ARE HYBRID FUNDS TAXED?

Taxation of Hybrid Funds have gone through major change from 1st April, 2023 after the changes announced by Finance Ministry as Budget 2023 Amendment.

Hybrid Funds can be taxed as per 3 slabs – Equity, Hybrid or Debt Taxation.

If a fund's portfolio is holding more than 65% of its assets as investments in the domestic equity market, then it is taxed as Equity Funds (More details in Q19). If a fund's portfolio is more than 35% and less than 65% of its assets as investments in the domestic equity market, it is taxed as earlier Debt Taxation (before 1st Apr 2023) and can be called as Hybrid Taxation i.e. at tax slab if holding period is less than 3 years and 20% with indexation benefit if holding period is above 3 years. If a fund's portfolios is less than 35% of its assets as investment in the domestic equity market, it is taxed as Debt funds (More details in Q33).

Now this allocation in equity market needn't be just buying of stocks, it can also include investing in Arbitrage opportunities (Derivatives) in Stock market where fund manager can take riskless positions by buying & selling same stock at same time in different indices or markets due to price mismatch. More details on Arbitrage in Q50.

Primarily, Arbitrage Funds, Balanced Advantage and Equity Savings Funds take the benefit of these Arbitrage investments to make sure their total Equity component is 65% and above and they are taxed as Equity Funds.

Taxation of Mutual Funds-Category Wise

श्री investyadnya.in   (On new investment on or after 1st April 2023)

	Debt	Hybrid	Equity
Equity %	0-35%	>35% and <65%	65% and above
STCG	Taxable at Tax Slab	Taxable at Tax Slab	15%
LTCG		20% with Indexation	10% Tax on Gain of >₹1 lakh in FY
Holding period to avail LTCG	Only STCG applied irrespective of holding period	3 Years and above	1 year and above
Category	-Debt mutual funds & ETFs -Gold funds and ETFs -International funds, ETFs, FOFs -Conservative hybrid funds(they hold maximum 25% in equities)	Balanced hybrid funds Balanced advantage funds or dynamic asset allocation funds or Multi Asset Funds These schemes strive to keep at least 65% of the total proceeds of the fund in domestic equity & equity related instruments (based on annual average of the monthly averages of opening and closing figures) to attract equity taxation benefits as per prevailing tax laws. In majority schemes, Equity or Hybrid Taxation will apply. Scheme wise variation will apply.	-Domestic equity mutual funds -Arbitrage Funds -Aggressive hybrid funds -Equity savings

How Hybrid Taxation works?

So, if the fund has lower than 65% Equity allocation but above 35% Equity allocation, it's gains will be treated like Debt Fund taxation before 1st April 2023 i.e.

	Holding Period	**Taxation**
Short Term Capital Gain	Less than 36 months	Gains added to your income of the year of redemption and taxed as per applicable tax slab
Long Term Capital Gain	More than 36 months	You will have to pay 20% tax on gains after Indexatio

Indexation means adjustment of gains with respect to Inflation i.e. subtracting the impact of inflation on your returns and then paying taxes. Inflation here is calculated based on CII (Cost Inflation Index) provided by Income tax department each year. Indexation is explained with example in Q33.

All the dividends on mutual funds are now taxed as per your Income tax slab.

45. WHAT ARE VARIOUS TYPES OF HYBRID FUNDS?

There are different types of hybrid Mutual Funds that invest in various equity, debt and other assets in different proportion. Below is the classification of Hybrid funds based on SEBI notification 'Categorization & Rationalization of Mutual Fund Schemes' dated October 6th, 2017.

Type of Debt Fund	**%age of Equity & Equity Related Instruments**	**% of Debt & Debt Related Instruments**	**Points to Note**
Conservative Hybrid Fund	10%-25%	75%-90%	Earlier known as MIP (Monthly Income Plans) Taxation as Debt Funds.

Aggressive Hybrid Fund	65%-80%	20%-35%	Earlier known as Balanced Funds. Taxation as Equity Funds.
Dynamic Asset Allocation or Balanced Advantage	Not fixed. Depends on Fund Manager's view of market. Can be 0-100%	Not fixed. Depends on Fund Manager's view of market. Can be 0-100%.	Should be managed similar to Aggressive Hybrid Category. Taxation depends on allocation but in all likelihood, fund managers will keep it as Equity.
Multi-Asset Allocation	Min. 10%	Min. 10%	Have to invest in min. 3 asset classes. Mostly they will take 3 assets as Equity, Debt & Gold with minimum 10% in each. Taxation depends on allocation but in all likelihood will be kept as Equity.
Arbitrage Funds	Min 65% (All Arbitrage Investments)	0-35%	Very low risk. Should be compared to Liquid Category Funds. Taxation as Equity. More details in Q50.
Equity Savings	Min 65% (Out of this, mostly carry 20%-30% Arbitrage Investments)	Min 10%	Real Equity component is mostly between 30-45% and rest is arbitrage to make it's taxation as Equity.
Balanced Hybrid Fund	40%-60% No Arbitrage Allowed	40%-60%	Not a popular category With changes in taxation and introduction of Hybrid Taxation, this category may gain prominence in future.

46.   WHAT ARE AGGRESSIVE HYBRID FUNDS?

Aggressive Hybrid funds are a combination of Debt and Equity funds. They were earlier known as Balanced Funds or Equity Oriented Hybrid Funds. They have equity as predominant portion of their portfolio accounting to 65-80%. Equity adds a considerable amount of risk to the product and debt helps in cushioning of the funds in case if equity asset class fails to perform.

These Funds are becoming very popular in last few years, majorly due to their profile of giving growth like Equity funds and cushioning of safer debt funds. The assets under management (AUM) of aggressive Hybrid funds has increased a lot in the last three years and have touched more than 1.7 Lakh Crores in Feb 2023 due to increased inflows and rising number of investors.

Example (Data as on 1st Feb, 2023)**:**

Biggest Aggressive Hybrid Fund by Asset under management is SBI Equity Hybrid Fund

Returns in Last 3 years: 10.9% p.a.

Returns in Last 5 years: 09.25% p.a.

Portfolio: 74.12% Equity and 25.88% Debt & Cash

47.   SHOULD I INVEST IN AGGRESSIVE HYBRID FUNDS?

Pros and Cons

Aggressive Hybrid are a great investment option for conservative Equity Investor or for early mutual fund investors. Let's understand their Pros and Cons before deciding if we should invest or not.

Advantages of Aggressive Hybrid Funds

Best of Both: Funds with exposure to both Equity and Debt brings best of both - the potential of higher returns from the equity component and stability of the debt component.

<u>Automatic Rebalancing</u>: Due to presence of both Equity and Debt, these funds sell equity at high (book profits) and buy at low to keep the share close to the objective.

<u>Less Volatile than Equity</u> due to presence of Debt portion.

<u>Tax Efficient</u>: Aggressive Hybrid Funds are treated same way as Equity Funds from Taxation point of view and therefore are very tax efficient

<u>Good Returns</u>: These Funds have given comparable returns to Equity in last few years. Their average returns are not too far from Large Cap Equity funds in last 3 years and 5 years.

Disadvantages of Aggressive Hybrid Funds

<u>Not Risk Free</u>: These Funds are certainly not risk free nor low risk like Debt Funds. Since more than 2/3rd of portfolio is in Equity, they do carry lot of volatility from stock markets.

<u>Interest Rate Risk</u>: Though at smaller level, they do carry interest rate risk as well, due to exposure to Debt instruments.

<u>Difficult to calculate Asset Allocation</u>: For investors who follow their asset allocation with discipline, they would find investing in Aggressive Hybrid Funds difficult as their Equity/Debt share changes very frequently, which makes calculation of exact asset allocation of your portfolio difficult.

<u>More dependence on Fund Manager</u> as he/she must have knowledge of both Equity and Debt markets and accordingly take calls to select best of both.

Our Take:

Aggressive Hybrid funds are a great product but need little more understanding as these are neither entirely equity and nor debt. We believe it is a good product to invest for your medium-term goals (3-5 years). It is also a good product for retirees who want some wealth creation for their extra assets, which wouldn't be used for long term.

48. WHAT ARE CONSERVATIVE HYBRID FUNDS?

Conservative Hybrid Funds, earlier known as Monthly Income Plans (MIP) or Debt Oriented Hybrid funds are a combination of Debt and Equity funds with a predominant portion of Debt accounting to 75-90% and a smaller allocation in equity securities (10% to 25%). As there is not much correlation between Equity and Debt markets, this product endeavours to give an investor, returns that are relatively higher than debt market returns.

Conservative Hybrid Funds can be called as debt oriented hybrids that seek to –

* Generate income from the debt securities
* Maximize the benefits of long term growth from equity securities

Key Features:

1. <u>No Guaranteed Regular Income</u>: The earlier name of these funds (MIP) may make you think that they give guaranteed monthly income, but that is not the case. Though major investment in debt part assures you some dividend but it is not guaranteed and nor it is fixed. During bad performance phase, you may not get any dividend at all.

2. <u>Interest rate and stock market risk</u>: Like Aggressive Hybrid funds, Conservative Hybrid Funds too, carry both interest rate and stock market risks but in different degree due to different exposures.

3. <u>Returns</u>: Average Trailing Conservative Hybrid fund returns in last 3 years have been around 11.5% p.a. (As on 1st April 23). These returns are resultant of 2021 equity market over performance but your long-term expectations from these funds should be 1-2% higher than Debt Funds returns.

4. <u>Taxation</u>: Their tax treatment is same as of Debt funds. You can get more details in *Q33*. In future, these funds taxation could be pushed to Hybrid Taxation (Q44) by adding Arbitrage to take total equity allocation to 35%.

5. <u>Who should Invest?</u>

    a. Retired or semi-retired investors looking for regular income should consider Conservative Hybrid Funds as an option.

    b. Conservative Investors who want extra returns: Investors who majorly invests in Debt options want to take marginally additional risk for some extra returns.

    c. High Risk Investors who want to invest for short term (<3 years) but want to take some extra risk can also choose these funds.

Example (Data as on 1st Feb 23): ICICI Pru Regular Savings Fund

Returns: Last 1 year: 4.63% | Last 3 years: 8.40% (Annualized)

Launched in 2004, Asset Allocation: Debt- 60.37%, Equity- 21.97% & Cash – 17.67%

49. DIFFERENCE BETWEEN CONSERVATIVE HYBRID FUNDS, MIS AND BANK FIXED DEPOSITS?

BASIS	Conservative Hybrid Funds (MIPs)	Bank Fixed Deposits	Post Office MIS
Definition	A Mutual Fund Scheme with 75-90% investments in Debt instruments and rest in Equity	Deposit scheme of Banks	Monthly Income Scheme of Post Office
Risk	Medium Risk as some part is invested in volatile Equity markets	Very Low	Very Low

Guaranteed Returns	No, depends on Stock market and Interest rate movement. SWP is the best option to get fixed monthly income.	Assured Returns	Assured Returns
Returns (Feb 2023)	High Returns as compared to others. Have given returns of 5-11% p.a. in last 3 years	Returns vary from 5%-6.5% p.a.	Current rate of interest is 7.1% p.a.
Maximum Investment Limit	No Limit	No Limit	₹4.5 Lacs for single account and ₹9 Lacs for joint account
Premature Withdrawals?	0%-1% of NAV would be deducted for up to 1 year depending on different funds	Mostly 1% reduction in the agreed upon interest rate	2% from the deposit would be deducted before 3 years and 1% after 3 years till maturity
Taxation	Returns as per your Tax slab. Same as Debt funds, refer Q33	Returns are taxed as per your tax slab	Returns are taxed as per your tax slab
TDS	No	Yes, if the interest earned is more than ₹40,000/year a TDS at 10% is levied if the PAN is provided and if it is not provided, 20% tax is levied for domestic deposits. In case of NRO deposits a TDS of 31.2% is applicable.	No

Our Take:

Conservative Hybrid Funds are a great tool for retired investors who have got a large lump sum amount. They should invest that money in these funds and take low risk as compared to other Equity products and get good and tax efficient returns. They should put a SWP on that amount if they need a fixed monthly income from it. Conservative Hybrid Funds are much more effective than Annuities, MISs and Fixed deposits from long term perspective (>3 years)

50. WHAT ARE ARBITRAGE FUNDS?

Before understanding the concept of these funds, we should know the definition of the word *'Arbitrage'*. Arbitrage is the simultaneous buying and selling of an asset in different markets to benefit from the price difference of the assets in those markets. It is a trade that produces risk free profits by exploiting the price difference of the same financial instrument on different markets or in different forms. Arbitrage exists due to market inefficiencies.

Example: Suppose Tata Motors stock is trading at ₹500 on the BSE while, at the same moment, it is trading for ₹500.10 on the NSE. A trader can buy the stock on the BSE and immediately sell the same shares on the NSE, earning a riskless profit of 10 paise per share. This risk-free profit is arbitrage.

In financial markets, these arbitrage opportunities may exist due to price difference between two indices, spot and future prices and currency exchanges. Arbitrage Funds majorly take the benefit of difference in spot and future price.

In Arbitrage funds, mutual fund manager looks for such Arbitrage opportunities i.e. mispricing between the cash markets or spot markets on one hand and derivatives or futures markets on the other.

Key Features of Arbitrage Funds-

1. Arbitrage Funds are safe and carry little risk. Fund manager reduces the risk of equity by hedging against

derivatives. Their returns are not impacted by Market volatility.

2. More the volatility in the market, more mispricing opportunities and hence better performance of Arbitrage Funds.

3. Since major portion of their portfolio is invested in Equity, they are considered as Equity funds from tax perspective. To know more about Equity Fund taxation, please see *Q19*.

4. Though their risk profile is similar to Debt Funds, they cannot be considered alternate to Debt Funds as they are minimally impacted by interest rate changes.

5. The returns on these funds are mainly dependent on the fund manager's ability to spot arbitrage opportunities. These opportunities are limited in the market and lately more arbitrage funds have come up in the market. Therefore, with more funds i.e. more money chasing these arbitrage opportunities, the returns can reduce.

Example: Kotak Equity Arbitrage Fund, Nippon India Arbitrage Fund

51. SHOULD I INVEST IN ARBITRAGE FUNDS?

PROS AND CONS

Arbitrage Funds have become popular in last few years. With the risk profile of a Debt fund and tax benefit of an Equity Funds, are these funds worth investing? Let's find out by understanding their Pros and Cons:

Pros of Arbitrage Funds

<u>Low Risk</u>: Since these funds operate on risk free profit from Arbitrage opportunities, they have a low risk profile equivalent to Liquid or Debt Funds.

<u>Tax Efficient</u>: Arbitrage Funds are treated as Equity Funds from tax perspective; so, you get long term capital gains just after a single year and not 3 years as in case of Debt Funds.

Cons of Arbitrage Funds

<u>Limited Opportunities</u>: There are limited arbitrage opportunities in the market. With increasing number of funds and money, benefits of these funds are reducing. The ability to generate returns comes down when more money chases the same arbitrage opportunities.

<u>Highly dependent on Fund Manager</u>: Since arbitrage opportunities exist for a very short time period, these funds need a skilful Fund manager who can exploit such opportunities before others do.

<u>Below Average Returns</u>: Performance of these funds is on decline as the money inflow is increasing in these funds. Increased inflow increases competition on limited arbitrage opportunities. Currently, their average 1, 3 & 5 year return is even less than Liquid Funds (as of Feb 2023)

Our Take:

You should avoid investing in Arbitrage Funds as their Disadvantages outweigh their Advantages unless you are in a high tax brackets. You may think about investing in them for short term (1-2 Years) and if you are in 30% tax bracket, then due to tax advantage they may prove to be beneficial. These perform well in a scenario when equity markets are highly volatile, interest rates are low (hence liquid funds give low returns) and inflation is high.

52. LIQUID FUND VS ARBITRAGE FUND

<u>Time horizon</u>: This is a very important constraint to know before investing. If one wants to invest for minimum 6 months, then arbitrage funds can be considered. Ideally, investment horizon for arbitrage funds should be more than 6 months as there can

be high short term volatility. For investment horizon ranging from few days to weeks, liquid funds are a good option.

Risk Factor: Liquid funds are considered to be much safer than arbitrage funds because they invest in debt instruments. Arbitrage funds are riskier as they invest their money in arbitrage opportunities of Equity Markets and many times enough arbitrage opportunities are not available or market sentiments are very weak and future market runs with discount. Arbitrage funds can give you negative returns too in very short term whereas Liquid Funds rarely do that.

Return on Investment: Due to limited arbitrage opportunities and too many funds chasing same opportunities, Liquid funds' returns have been better than Arbitrage Funds in last few years. Following table shows the returns for various holding periods

As of 16th Jan 2023:

Holding Period	Arbitrage Funds	Liquid Funds
1 Day	0.08%	0.01%
1 Week	0.13%	0.09%
1 Month	0.60%	0.45%
3 Months	1.40%	1.40%
1 Year	4.12%	4.31%
3 Years	3.74%	3.50%
5 Years	4.45%	4.75%
10 Years	6.02%	6.53%

Liquidity: Liquid funds provide far better liquidity as compared to arbitrage funds. It takes transaction day+3 days to redeem an arbitrage fund while liquid funds can be encashed within a day. Liquid funds with instant redemption option can be redeemed within minutes.

Expense Ratio: On an average, expense ratio of liquid funds (Direct Plan) is 0.15 while that of arbitrage funds (Direct Plan)

is about 0.40. Expense ratio of arbitrage funds is high due to number of transactions and cost associated with it. On this factor, Liquid funds score better.

Exit Load: Exit load is the fees charged by the Asset Management Company (AMC) at the time of redemption. AMCs charge 0.25% to 0.50% for arbitrage funds if redeemed within one month. Mostly it is 0.25%. For Liquid Funds, Exit load is very low, here are the details

Redemption Day	Exit Load for liquid funds
On first day	0.0070%
On second day	0.0065%
On third day	0.0060%
On fourth day	0.0055%
On fifth day	0.0050%
On sixth day	0.0045%
On or After seventh day	Nil

Tax: There is a major difference in taxation of liquid funds and arbitrage funds. For taxation purpose, arbitrage funds are treated as equity funds and they attract flat 15% tax on the short term capital gains if sold before one year. And 10% if sold after 1 year. Capital gains on Liquid funds are taxed as per tax slab if the investment is done after 1st April 2023 (Check Q33 of detailed). For investor in high tax brackets, investment in liquid funds would not be attractive.

Conclusion: Overall, both liquid funds and arbitrage funds have their own advantages and disadvantages depending on the type of investor. If you are an investor in high tax brackets, then only you should consider Arbitrage Funds as an investment.

53. WHAT ARE EQUITY SAVINGS FUND? SHOULD I BUY IT?

One of a relatively new entrants in hybrid funds category is equity savings fund. Budget 2014 increased the minimum holding period for non-equity funds to qualify for long term capital gain taxation from 12 months to 36 months, thereby reducing the attractiveness of debt funds. This created a new category called Equity Savings Funds which has now been formalized in the SEBI's new categorization. Equity savings funds try to balance risk and returns by investing in equity, debt and derivatives.

The basic idea is that they invest a third in equity, a third in arbitrage and a third in fixed income. The risk profile is debt but their tax profile is that of equity (as Arbitrage + Equity is above 65%). These can be considered as conservative hybrid funds which are treated as equity funds from a taxation point of view. Conservative Hybrid Funds don't go beyond 25% in equity, but these funds are mostly around 33% in equity and can go even higher and depends on fund to fund.

Example (As of Feb 2023) – Nippon Equity Savings Fund has Equity allocation of upto 38% whereas Kotak Equity Savings fund has 33% allocation in Equity.

Should I buy? – From Risk profile, these funds sit between Conservative Hybrid Funds and Aggressive Hybrid Funds with benefit of equity taxation. These funds are a good option for investors looking to invest in Conservative Hybrid Funds and fall in higher tax brackets (20% & 30%). Ideal funds for high risk investors who are planning to invest for their short term goals (2-4 years). They are also a good option for conservative investors who think Aggressive hybrid funds are too risky.

54. DIFFERENCE BETWEEN BALANCED ADVANTAGE FUNDS & MULTI ASSET ALLOCATION? WHICH ONE IS FOR ME?

These are two new categories formalized by SEBI in their new fund categorization circular dated Oct 6, 2017. These categories used to exist earlier as well but there were very few serious funds but now with new rationalization, some very big funds have been allocated to these two categories and hence these categories have assumed prominence. Let's discuss the difference and understand which one is for us –

Basis	Dynamic Asset Allocation	Multi Asset Allocation
Definition	Investment in equity/ debt that is managed dynamically. Also called a Balanced Advantage Fund (BAF)	Invests in at least three asset classes with a minimum allocation of atleast 10% each in all three asset classes (Equity, Debt and Gold (mostly))
Risk	Lower than Aggressive Hybrid Funds, higher than other Hybrids: Since allocation can be dynamically managed from 0-100% in Equity or 0-100% in debt, fund manager can take allocation based on different market performances	Similar to dynamic asset allocation. Additional asset (mostly Gold) could bring its own extra risk but could be beneficial as well as it sometime act as a good hedge to Equity.
Diversification	Very good diversification – Diversified across Equity & Debt portfolio	Even more diversification – Apart from Equity & Debt, it is mandated to invest in one more asset class (Real Estate, Gold etc) which help in highest level of diversification in domestic market.
Returns	Both are new categories, tough to comment. Depends a lot on the fund manager and his/her allocation calls. But mostly should be comparable to Aggressive Hybrid Funds.	
Taxation	Taxation of both these categories should depend on their Equity allocation in the year. If average Equity allocation has been above 65%, then the fund will be taxed as per Equity taxation, if it is between 35% to 65%, then Hybrid, otherwise as Debt. Equity allocation will be calculated based on average daily equity allocation in the Financial Year. To understand this better, check Q44 We believe, all BAF would surely try to maintain allocation of above 65% to get equity taxation advantage but things could be different in Multi Asset allocation and could largely depend on fund manager and fund house strategy.	

Example	HDFC Prudence Fund (earlier a Balanced Fund) has converted to HDFC Balanced Advantage Fund (close to ₹51k Cr AUM as of Feb 2023) but fund has maintained its earlier aggressive hybrid strategy (more than 65% allocation to Equity) ICICI Pru Balanced Advantage Fund (Close to ₹45k Cr AUM as of Feb 2023) is now been tagged to this category. It keeps its Equity allocation around 45% and 20% in arbitrage to keep taxation as Equity	ICICI Pru Multi Asset Fund (more than ₹16k Cr AUM as of Feb 2023) is tagged to this category (Earlier known as ICICI Pru Dynamic Plan). This fund has always kept its Equity allocation more than 65% to keep Equity taxation.

Our Take:

These two categories give lot more power to Fund Managers. They can dynamically change their allocation between two categories (Equity & Debt) in Balanced Advantage Funds and between three categories (Equity, Debt, Commodity) in Multi-Asset Allocation based on market conditions. A good fund manager can help you reduce the market risk by changing the portfolio based on his future market expectations whereas a bad fund manager can increase the risk. Our view is that you should check the history on how Fund Managers manages the fund in these categories. Every Fund manager may have a very different strategy within this category like ICICI Pru Balanced Adv is managed more like Equity Savings Category Funds whereas HDFC Pru Balanced Adv is managed more like Aggressive Hybrid Category. Choose the Fund manager rather than the category.

CATEGORY 6

Sector or Thematic Funds

"Risk comes from not knowing what you are doing, so wide diversification is only required when investors are ignorant. You only have to do a very few things in life so long as you don't do too many things wrong"

–Warren Buffett

55. WHAT ARE SECTORAL or THEMATIC FUNDS?

Sectoral or Thematic funds a type of mutual fund, which invest solely in businesses that operate in an industry or sector or a theme of the economy. Because all holdings of this type of fund are in the same industry or theme, there is an inherent lack of diversification associated with these funds. Also, risk levels of these funds depend on the risk of the industry sector or the theme. These funds are mandated to invest minimum 80% in the underlying sector or theme. Commonly, sectoral or thematic funds focus on - Banking & Financial Services, Infrastructure, Technology, Pharma, MNC companies, FMCG and Real Estate.

Unlike other categories, where a fund house is mandated to keep maximum one fund in the category, there is no limit on number of Sectoral or Thematic funds a fund house can have.

Example: UTI Banking sector fund, ICICI Pru Technology Fund, Aditya Birla SL MNC Fund

56. WHAT ARE DIFFERENT TYPES OF SECTORAL OR THEMATIC FUNDS IN INDIAN MARKET?

There are various types of sector funds which exist in Indian market:

1. Banking: These funds invest in Banking and Financial Sector. They are the most popular Sector funds in India. There are around 15 Banking sector funds currently in Indian market. For **Example:** SBI Banking & Financial Services Fund.

2. Infrastructure: These funds invest majorly in capital goods companies which help in infrastructure growth of the country. There are around 19 Infrastructure fund options available to invest. For **Example:** UTI Infrastructure Fund.

3. <u>Pharma</u>: They invest in stocks of Pharmaceutical or Healthcare companies. These funds became very popular in early part of this decade as the pharma sector gave extraordinary returns. There are total 10 funds focusing exclusively on this sector. For **Example:** Nippon India Pharma Fund.

4. <u>Technology</u>: These funds invest in the technology or technology dependent companies. Currently, there are 5 such funds in Indian market. **Example:** ICICI Pru Technology Fund.

5. <u>FMCG</u>: These funds invest in Consumer Good companies. There are 6 funds dedicated to this sector. **Example:** SBI Consumption Opportunities Fund.

6. <u>Other Themes</u>: There are few other themes as well, such as:

   a. <u>MNC</u>: This fund invests only in multinational companies listed in Indian stock exchange. **Example:** Aditya Birla SL MNC Fund.

   b. <u>Energy</u>: These funds invest in Energy and Power sector. **Example:** Nippon India Power & Infra Fund.

   c. <u>PSU</u>: These funds invest only in Public Sector companies. **Example:** SBI PSU Fund.

   d. <u>Consumption</u>: They invest in consumption-oriented sectors (Automobile, Entertainment, FMCG etc). **Example:** Mirae Asset Great Consumer Fund

   e. <u>Automobile</u>: These funds invest in Automobile and ancillary sector companies. **Example:** UTI Transportation & Logistic Fund.

   f. <u>Ethical</u>: These funds invest in Sharia Compliant equity investments. **Example:** Tata Ethical Fund

g. <u>ESG</u>: These funds invest in companies by following Environmental, Social and Governance criteria. **Example**: SBI Magnum Equity ESG Fund.

h. <u>Quant</u>: These funds follow quant models (Algorithm based) of investing rather than depending on human expertise in fund management. **Example**: DSP Quant Fund, Tata Quant Fund.

i. <u>Business Cycle</u>: These Funds track cyclicity in the sector, business & economy and invest accordingly. **Example**: HSBC Business Cycle Fund.

j. <u>Manufacturing</u>: These Funds invest in Manufacturing based companies taking benefit of Make in India initiatives of GoI. **Example:** Kotak Manufacture in India Fund

57. SHOULD I INVEST IN SECTORAL OR THEMATIC FUNDS?

Pros & Cons

Sector funds are highly focused as they aim to invest in an industry or a sector. Their basic objective is to allow investors to take advantage of industry cycles.

Pros of Sectoral/Thematic Funds

<u>Burst of Outperformance</u>: Sector funds may give you extraordinary returns. As the saying goes, higher the risk, better could be the returns. For **example,** Returns of Nippon India Pharma Fund in past 3 years was 23.94% CAGR (as on 27th May 2022). However, from 1st July 2015 to 2nd July 2018 the fund posted a return of -3.4% whereas Nifty gave +10% returns between same period.

Cons of Sectoral/Thematic Funds

<u>Higher Risk</u>: Since the funds have complete exposure to one sector or theme, you take higher risk than other Equity Funds.

Taking an example, one small govt. regulation change can impact your investments immensely.

<u>Market Timing is important</u>: Since many industries perform in cycles, your investment timing becomes very important for these funds. Most difficult part is to know the right time.

<u>Limited Options for Fund manager</u>: Finding many good companies in a sector or theme could be a difficult task and therefore Fund Manager sometimes end up taking more risk than usual by investing in not so good ones or taking over exposure in few good ones.

<u>Correlation</u>: If you invest in the same sector fund where you work, you end up taking more risk as, if the sector is going through a rough patch, your returns as well as your income growth both may get impacted.

Our Take:

Sector or Thematic funds are one of the riskiest mutual funds due to exposure to few selected sectors but they have given outstanding returns too. We believe these funds are for high risk takers, who have extra disposable income. Alternatively, these funds are for those who understand and follow that sector/theme well.

CATEGORY 7

ETFs & Index Funds

"Stock Market is a device for transferring money from impatient to the patient"

–Warren Buffet

58. WHAT IS AN ETF?

ETF stands for Exchange traded fund. These are a type of investment funds that tracks an index, a commodity, bonds or basket of assets. The ETFs trading value is based on the net asset value of the underlying assets that it represents. Think of it as a Mutual Fund that you can buy and sell in real-time at a price that changes throughout the day. ETFs typically have higher daily liquidity and lower fees than mutual funds, making them an attractive alternative for individual investors.

In some sense the ETF is like a stock, as they are traded on the exchange on real-time basis, and thus needs a demat account for trade. In another sense, they work like Mutual funds as the underlying asset comprises of a set of stock/assets.

Functionality	ETF	Stock	MF
Real Time Pricing	✓	✓	X
Ability to put limit orders	✓	✓	X
Online Trade through Exchange	✓	✓	X
Diversification possible through a single unit purchase	✓	X	✓
Return at par with market/Index	✓	X	X
Exit Load	X	X	✓
Arbitrage possible between Future and Cash market	✓	✓	X

Example: UTI Gold ETF, SBI Sensex ETF

59. WHAT ARE VARIOUS TYPES OF ETFs AVAILABLE?

1) <u>Index ETF</u>: Oldest and most common type of ETFs today. They acquire stocks/shares in amounts that proportionately reflect an existing stock index. Goal of the fund is to emulate the index it reflects and not outperform it.

   Example: ICICI Prudential Nifty ETF reflects Nifty 50 Index

2) <u>Strategic ETF</u>: NSE & BSE has launched various strategic indices such as Nifty Alpha, Nifty Low Volatility, Nifty 50 Value 20, BSE Midcap Select etc. These indices work on specific formula/algo designed by NSE/BSE and have given some good performances. Many ETFs have launched based on these strategic Indices and have given good option to investors.

   Example: Nippon India ETF Nifty 50 Value 20, Kotak Nifty Alpha 50, SBI Quality ETF.

3) <u>Commodity ETF</u>: These ETFs invest in commodities such as Gold, Silver etc. Currently, only Gold ETFs are available in India. Prices of Gold ETFs move hand in hand with Physical Gold.

   Example: Nippon ETF Gold BeES

4) <u>Bond ETF</u>: These ETFs invest in bonds. When the stock market shows its downward swing, these ETFs are in demand.

   Example: LIC MF G-Sec Long-Term ETF which reflects Nifty 8-13 years G-Sec Index

5) <u>International ETFs</u>: These ETFs invest in Foreign index such as MSCI global index, NASDAQ etc.

   Example: Motilal Oswal NASDAQ 100 ETF, which reflects Nasdaq 100 index.

Index ETFs & Strategic ETFs are taxed similar to Equity Funds discussed in *Q19* whereas rest are taxed similar to Debt funds discussed in *Q33*.

60. HOW ETFs WORK? What is iNAV?

ETFs are created by Mutual Fund House (AMCs). They create the ETF units based on the demand during NFO. These units are then traded on exchange with AMCs having power to create more unit if buy demand is more or buy units (and exhume them) if not enough buyers are there in the market. AMCs also has to appoint two market makers for ETFs. The job of market makers is to again ensure that there's enough liquidity on the exchanges for ETFs by simultaneously providing buy and sell quotes.

The ETF market price is the price at which an ETF can be bought or sold on the exchanges during trading hours. If more buyers than sellers arise, the price will rise in the market, and the price will decline if more sellers appear. The net asset value (NAV) of an ETF represents the value of each share of the fund's underlying assets and cash at the end of the trading day. An ETF is said to trade at a premium when its price exceeds its NAV. An ETF is said to trade at a discount when its price is below its NAV.

iNAV provides an intraday indicative Net Asset Value of an ETF based on the market values of its underlying constituents. It is available on respective AMC's website. iNAV is reported approximately every 10-15 seconds, hence it represents a near real-time view of the value of a fund. Reporting an INAV can help a fund to avoid significant premium and discount trading. You should always check iNAV before buying or selling ETF. If market price is close to iNAV, then only you should execute the trade.

There have been many instances when iNAV and market price of ETF had big difference. Example when Mirae Asset NYSE FANG Plus ETF was launched, there was huge demand for the ETF and hence ETF was consistently trading at premium i.e. much higher over its iNAV.

ETF Trading on Premium & Discount is different than Tracking error of the fund. Tracking error is the difference between the returns of the fund and its benchmark index it is trying to mimic. A higher tracking error shows that the fund is not replicating the index truly. Recently in 2022, many International Fund ETFs had high tracking error as RBI had placed restrictions for

Mutual Funds on buying International stocks as the threshold for maximum investment allowed was reached. Due to this restrictions, Tracking error of many International Funds and ETFs increased as they couldn't mimic changes in the international portfolios due to restrictions in buying International Stocks.

61. SHOULD I INVEST IN ETF?

Pros & Cons

ETFs are a kind of Passively managed mutual funds. Just like any other investment vehicle, exchange-traded funds have their own benefits and drawbacks. So, before you invest in them, you need to know their pros and cons and decide if ETFs are the right option for you.

Pros of ETF

Lower Cost: Since they are passively managed, major benefit of ETFs is their very low cost structure. Their expense ratios are as low as only 0.07%.

Lower Risk: ETFs follow an index and hence are not dependent on a Fund Manager's decision making. Therefore, these are one of the least risky Equity funds.

Diversification: ETFs give you instant diversification in all stocks of the underlying Index.

Transparent Portfolio: ETFs have a very transparent portfolio holding and predefined basket creation.

You can time the market: Since ETFs can be traded actively like stocks, there is an option to time the market in case of wide intraday fluctuations.

Can start at very low investments: You can buy as low as 1 unit of ETF, which is typically for a few hundred rupees.

Easy to choose: Since ETFs simply track an index, you just need to finalize the type of index you want to buy.

Cons of ETF

<u>Trading costs can be high</u>: Depending on your brokerage plan esp. if you are buying and selling ETF frequently.

<u>Liquidity Risk</u>: Especially in Index ETFs, liquidity can be a risk as they are still not very popular in India. Still there are days when no trading happens in few of ETFs. Always check Trading volume & iNAV before investing in ETFs.

<u>Limited Options in India</u>: In developed Financial Markets, there is a wide variety of ETFs available such as – Currency ETF, Sector specific ETF, Active Managed ETF etc. which are not available in India

You <u>need to have a Demat account</u> to buy ETFs, you cannot buy them from your mutual fund account.

Our Take:

ETFs should definitely be part of your asset consideration. With new strategic indices based ETFs and launch of various sector and international ETFs, investors are getting decent choices with good performances too. Large Cap Funds can be replaced with ETFs looking at options, performances, liquidity and cost. Options in Small & midcap are still limited and have higher liquidity risks too.

62. WHAT ARE INDEX FUNDS?

Index funds are mutual funds, which follow indices like BSE Sensex and Nifty. These funds are passively managed funds and their performance is judged purely on replication of an index. They are similar to Index ETFs. Suppose we launch Yadnya Index fund – Sensex Plan. In that case, we would simply have to look at the 30 stocks of the BSE Sensex and invest the money in them in the same proportion as it is there in the index.

Example: ICICI Pru Nifty Next 50 Index Fund, HDFC Index Fund-Sensex etc.

63. SHOULD I INVEST IN INDEX FUNDS?

Pros and Cons

Before we decide, let's understand the Pros and Cons first:

Pros of Index Funds

Lower Cost: Major benefit of Index Funds is their very low cost structure. Their expense ratios are among the lowest among Equity Funds, it ranges from 0.3%-1%.

Lower Risk: Index Funds follow an index and hence are not dependent on Fund Manager's decision making. No biasness. Therefore, these are one of the least risky Equity funds.

Diversification: Index Funds give you instant diversification in all stocks of the underlying Index.

Easy to choose: Since Index Funds simply track an index, you just need to finalize a fund with least tracking error.

Cons of Index Funds

Lesser Flexibility: Fund Manager just has to follow the changes in Index; he/she does not have any flexibility to change the portfolio.

Average Returns: These are not very popular in India, as most of the active fund managers easily beat Index returns. But things are looking better in future.

Stuck with certain stocks even though they are out of favour: Till the time leading Index holds these stocks, you are stuck with these even though you know these are not going to perform.

Our Take:

Index funds are for investors who are looking for comparatively lower risk Equity product which has a low cost. Good for first time Equity investors.

64. INDEX FUNDS V/S ETF?

Basis	Index Funds	ETFs
Structure	These keep higher percentage of assets as Cash and equivalent to manage redemptions etc. This leaves tracking error, higher the error greater the deviation from Index returns.	These too hold some cash or equivalent for liquidity but it is much lesser than Index Funds. These track the Index more efficiently than Index Funds.
Transaction	You can buy or sell them like any other mutual fund. You can also do systematic transactions (SIP, STP, SWP)	As the name suggests, they are bought and sold on exchange and need a Demat account to execute transaction. Systematic transactions are difficult to implement on ETFs.
Charges	Though lesser than other Equity Funds, they do have some fund management charges like other Mutual Funds, which you must incur yearly.	ETFs have almost negligible fund management charges and you just need to pay your regular brokerage and Demat account charges, which mostly is lesser than Index Funds unless you buy & sell ETFs too many times.
Liquidity	No liquidity risk as Fund house would invest directly in the underlying index stocks	High liquidity risk as one ETF unit is bought and sold as single stock and since ETFs are not very popular in India, trading volumes are very low which leads to liquidity risk.

Our Take:

If you must choose between these two, we would suggest going for Index Funds just because they offer the option to invest through SIP or STP even though they are little costly than ETFs. We strongly believe Systematic way is a great way to invest money in Equity markets as it creates an investment discipline and reduces short term market risk. Index Funds also has No Liquidity risk which is available in ETFs.

65. WHAT ARE DEBT ETFS? HOW THEY WORK?

The Bharat Bond ETFs are India's first corporate debt ETFs. Companies approach the firm managing the bond ETF with their borrowing requirements. The bond ETF raises funds from investors and hands them over to the underlying companies for a fixed tenure. Once the tenure is over, these companies return the amounts back to the ETF, which then passes it on to the investors. The units of the ETFs will be listed on the stock exchanges where they can be traded. Bharat Bond ETFs currently have PSU bonds only and we are sure more such ETFs will be launched in near future with wider corporate bonds.

The corporate bond market, where NCDs and other debt instruments are issued by companies, remains fairly illiquid. That is, there aren't enough buyers and sellers of these securities in the secondary market and therefore price discovery for such bonds become complicated. Now, with Debt ETFs corporates will collectively issue fresh securities. The ETF also can pick up already-issued and existing securities of the same companies with the same maturity and converts them into an investment basket. As the ETF units are bought and sold (similar to Equity ETFs), the underlying securities too get traded (through the market makers that the fund house appoints) and thereby become more liquid.

Specifically, Bharat Bond ETFs, do not carry credit risk. These invest in only AAA-rated State-owned firms.

Case of Rating downgrade or default - The bond ETF needs to be agile if an underlying company defaults on its interest or principal payments, or even if its credit rating falls. If a company gets downgraded, but still remains an investment-grade paper, the indices will remove the security at the subsequent rebalancing date. The ETF will also simultaneously exit the security. But between the downgrade and the exit, the security's price can drastically go down and impact the scheme's net asset value.

If the underlying security defaults, then there's a bigger problem. ETF will remove a defaulting security, but at a price that is found reasonable. This can cause a setback to the fund, though in case of Bharat Bond ETF, state-owned AAA-rated defaulting is a rare occurrence. Bharat Bond ETF has a provision for a segregated portfolio, like most other open-ended debt funds.

<u>Should you invest?</u>

The USP of such launches is that if held to maturity (Target Maturity Funds), these funds mimic fixed deposits (FDs). They pay a predictable (though not guaranteed) rate of return. The return, roughly speaking, is the yield of the fund minus its expense ratio. Expense ratio is also very less.

Many Debt Index Funds & ETFs are live & in pipeline after the success of Bharat Bond ETF.

66. WHAT ARE GOLD ETFS? BENEFITS OVER PHYSICAL GOLD?

Gold ETF are a type of Exchange Traded Fund, which represents Physical Gold in paper or demat form. As the name says, Gold ETFs are open-ended mutual fund schemes which invest money collected from investors, in standard gold bullion (0.995 purity). The investor's holding is denoted in units, which is listed on a stock exchange and follows the daily fluctuation of Gold's prices. Each unit of ETF approximately represents 1gm of Gold.

Key Features:

1. Most popular ETF schemes in India
2. No Lock in period, you can redeem your investments anytime

3. Taxed in the same way as Debt Funds i.e. as per tax slabs if invested after 1st April 2023, as explained in *Q33*

4. A gold ETF invests 90-100 per cent in physical gold sourced from the RBI approved banks and 0-10 per cent in debt instruments to meet any redemption needs

Example: UTI Gold ETF, Kotak Gold ETF Fund

Here is the comparison of Gold ETFs and Physical Gold -

Basis	Gold ETFs	Physical Gold
Risk	No storage risk and associated storage cost. No Purity Risk	Physical Gold has both storage and purity risk
Mode of Investment	You need to have a demat account to buy Gold ETF	You can buy gold from any bank or jewellery shop
Charges	Expense ratio of up to 0.3% on your investments and ETF transaction cost (Demat cost)	Though there are no management charges but other charges such as Storage charges, insurance charges, quality assurance charges, making charges etc. are involved
Liquidity	Gold ETFs are highly liquid as investors can sell it at any time on the exchange	Physical Gold can be difficult to sell and may not get the right price

67. GOLD ETFS V/S GOLD SAVINGS FUNDS V/S SOVEREIGN GOLD SCHEME?

Basis	Gold ETFs	Gold Funds	Sovereign Gold Bonds (SGB)
Where do they invest?	Physical Gold kept in safe & insured vaults	Gold Funds invest in Gold ETFs	They are bonds issued by RBI on behalf of Govt. of India to reduce Gold Imports and raise capital
Interest Rate	None	None	Govt. gives fixed interest rate of 2.5% p.a. on initial holding payable semi-annually. This interest rate is irrespective of Gold Price fluctuations.

Sovereign Guarantee	None	None	Yes
Asset Allocation	90-100% Gold 0-10% Debt to manage redemptions	95-100% Gold ETF 0-5% Cash/cash equivalent	100% Gold
Purity	.995	.995	.999
How to buy?	Demat Required	Mutual Fund account or Demat	Can subscribe through any bank or post office. Can also buy online through internet banking or demat account.
Investment Limits	Minimum 1 unit i.e. 1 gm of Gold	Min. ₹ 5000	Min. 1 unit i.e. 1 gm of gold and max 500 gm is allowed (For individuals)
Availability	Can buy anytime	Can buy anytime	Can be subscribed only during certain time window called Series. Series is open for 5 days. There are about 10-14 series every year.
SIP	Mostly not allowed	Allowed	Not Applicable
Listed	On Stock Exchange	N/A	On Stock Exchange. Can be purchased and sold on exchange but liquidity is low
Lock in Period	None	No Lock-in and you can take out money anytime but Exit load charged is up to 1% for redemptions within 1 year	Maturity period of 8 years but you can do early exit after 5 years. Can also be traded on Commodity exchange.

Cost and Charges	Expense Ratio of up to 1% chargeable each year. Over this there will also be brokerage charges.	Up to 0.3% of Fund Management charges over ETF's expense ratio. So, total expenses of up to 1.3% per annum	No charges. All the distribution and other expenses to be borne by Govt.
Loan Against	N/A	N/A	Loan against SGBs can be availed from banks
Taxation	Gains are taxed as per tax slab.	If holding period is above 3 years, taxation will be 20% after indexation benefit	If you hold these bonds till the maturity (8 years), no capital gains tax is payable. But you need to pay tax based on your slab on the interest income you get

Our Take:

If you need to invest in Gold, SGBs score on all aspects – less cost, extra interest and more tax efficient. SGB is the by far the best way to invest in Gold, only disadvantage is that you cannot invest systematically and scheme is available only during certain period to buy.

CATEGORY 8

Other Type of Mutual Funds

"In choosing a portfolio, investors should seek broad diversification, Further, they should understand that equities--and corporate bonds also--involve risk; that markets inevitably fluctuate; and their portfolio should be such that they are willing to ride out the bad as well as the good times."

–Harry Markowitz

68. WHAT IS ELSS OR TAX SAVING MUTUAL FUNDS?

ELSS is a type of diversified equity mutual fund, which is qualified for tax exemption under section 80C of the Income Tax Act. It comes with a lock-in period of three years. There are more than 39 ELSS schemes as of Feb 23 available in the Mutual Fund market, with almost ₹1,50,000 Crore worth assets under management.

Key points to note:

1. Try to avoid last minute lump sum investments in ELSS funds as they are linked to Equity markets just like other Equity Funds. It is always better to start investing in them in systematic way from the start of a Financial year.

2. You should invest in ELSS funds against your long-term financial goals only. Though these funds have lock-in of three years, you should stay invested even after three years' period is over. You should redeem these investments only when the goal is near.

3. Many advisors recommend investing in ELSS funds even if Section 80C 1.5 Lakhs limit is reached as the performance of these funds is as good as other large cap or flexi cap equity funds.

4. Please take extra care while selecting ELSS funds as, even though they are put in the same basket of Tax Planning, some of these funds maybe more large cap oriented and others maybe small/mid-cap oriented. So, select a fund, which suits your risk profile and/ or investment horizon.

5. Always buy Growth plan of ELSS funds as dividend re-investment plan (Now known as 'Reinvestment of Income distribution cum capital withdrawal plan (R-IDCW)) will make taxation complicated.

6. SEBI has now allowed fund house to launch an Index Fund as ELSS Fund too from Jan 2023. IIFL ELSS Nifty 50 Tax Saver Index Fund is first such fund to be launched in Jan 2023 with is a Nifty 50 Index Fund in ELSS category with very low expense ratio of only 0.27% (Direct Plan)

Examples: Franklin India Taxshield Fund is conservative in approach with most allocation to large caps, Axis Long Term Equity Fund has a balanced approach and has some mid/small-cap allocation too whereas Aditya Birla Sunlife Tax Relief 96 is an aggressive ELSS fund with higher allocation to mid/small caps as of Dec 22.

69. ELSS v/s PPF v/s NSC v/s BANK FDS?

From Tax Saving u/s Section 80c perspective

Basis	ELSS	PPF	NSC	Bank FDs
Lock In	Only 3 Years	15 Years	5 Years	5 Years
Taxation	Taxable – Flat 10% on Gains. Gains above 1 lac are taxed.	Tax Free	Taxable as per Slab	Taxable as per slab
Risk	Highest Risk among all options as your money is invested in stocks listed on stock exchange	Very Safe with Sovereign Guarantee	Safe	Safe
Returns	Not Fixed: Linked to Equity Markets. Last 3 years trailing avg. returns: 13.7% p.a. Last 5 years trailing avg. returns: 8.33% p.a. (As on Feb 23)	Fixed: Govt. is giving 7.1% p.a. on your investments as of Feb 23	Fixed: Rate of interest is 7.0% p.a. as of Feb 23	Fixed: 6.0%-7.00% p.a. depending on Bank as of Feb 23

Our Take:

If you are a young and/or a risk-taking investor, ELSS should be your preferred mode of section 80c tax saving investment, due to their higher returns & lower tax implications.

70. WHAT IS A FUND OF FUNDS (FOF) SCHEME?

Fund of Funds is a type of mutual fund scheme that invests in funds of other mutual fund house or in schemes or funds of the same mutual fund house rather than directly in stocks, bonds and other securities. It is also called Multi Manager Investment.

Conceptually, it does what you as a retail investor would do; create a portfolio which contains several funds. The difference being, when you buy funds yourself, you buy them individually and hold and track them separately, while when you buy a fund of funds, you hold just one fund which in turn holds other mutual funds.

Example: Quantum Equity FoF Fund (Direct)

Expense Ratio (Over & above individual fund's expense ratio): 0.51%

5 Year Returns: 9.69% p.a. as of Nov 22

Last three year return: 14.87% (p.a) as of Nov 22

Exit Load: Nil for 10% units and 1% for remaining units on redemption on/within 365 days

Portfolio (Oct 22):

Fund Name	% Assets
Mirae Asset Large Cap Fund	12.34
Invesco India Midcap Fund	11.15
IIFL Focused Equity Fund	10.87
Sundaram Large and Mid Cap Fund	10.69
Canara Robeco Emerging Equities	10.67
Canara Robeco Bluechip Equity Fund	10.57
UTI Flexi Cap Fund	10.44
Invesco India Contra Fund	10.23
Kotak Flexicap Fund	10.02
Invesco India Growth Opportunities Fund	10.57

71. SHOULD I INVEST IN FOF?

Pros and Cons

Fund of funds can act as alternate to your mutual fund distributor as they help you maintain asset allocation as well as hold a portfolio of Mutual Funds with minimal effort.

Pros of FoF

<u>Highest Diversification</u>: Funds of Funds provide the highest level of diversification. By investing in different mutual funds not necessarily from same Fund house, a FoF gives diversification not just from type of assets but also from fund manager risk, fund house risk, etc.

<u>Experts to select Funds</u>: Expert fund managers select the funds for you with the sole objective to maximize Return/Risk ratio.

<u>Cost effective Asset allocation</u>: Fund houses do not have to pay taxes for switching the money among funds to rebalance the portfolio. If you rebalance your portfolio yourself, you are liable to pay capital gains tax.

<u>Less tracking</u>: Easy tracking of your overall portfolio, just buy and keep a track of one fund. There is no need to track different funds.

<u>Access to Institutional plans</u>: These funds help you to invest in Institutional plans of mutual funds in which you cannot invest directly or there is a high entry barrier.

Cons of FoF

<u>Extra Fees</u>: Major drawback is that FoF charges their own fees in addition to expense ratio of the funds they buy. Suppose average expense ratio of 5 funds in the portfolio is 1.2% and the expense ratio of FoF is 0.7% then you take a hit of total 1.9%.

<u>Tracking of holdings can be difficult</u>: Since each FoF holds 3-7 different mutual funds, tracking of individual stock holding with you, can be a tedious task.

<u>Debt fund like Taxation</u>: All FoFs must follow Debt Funds (Q33) like taxation even though they invest primarily in Equity schemes. As we know, equity schemes are more tax efficient and therefore this becomes FoFs' biggest disadvantage.

<u>Limited Options</u>: Most of the existing FoFs only invest in their own Fund house's fund scheme, which hampers diversification and limits the choice of selection of Funds. There are very few which invest in other Fund house's schemes as well, such as Quantum Equity FoF Fund, Aditya Birla Sun Life Asset Allocator Multi-Manager FoF, Aditya Birla Sun Life Financial Planning Fund FoF, etc

Our Take:

Fund of fund schemes are for investors who are not well versed with Mutual Fund schemes and do not have enough time to maintain the right asset allocation or track the schemes. These schemes are for investors who are clear about their financial objectives and asset allocation they want. But taxation like debt funds and extra expense ratio deter investors to invest in them. You should avoid them due to high taxation.

72. WHAT ARE CAPITAL PROTECTION FUNDS?

Capital Protection Funds (CPOF) are closed ended mutual funds with an objective of capital protection. This means they invest majority of their assets in debt instruments (around 80%) which have tenure equal to that of the scheme. Then they also seek capital appreciation by limited exposure (around 20%) to Equity or equity related instruments. From asset allocation perspective, they are like Conservative Hybrid Funds discussed in Q48, major difference being that Conservative Hybrid Funds are open Ended and CPOFs are closed ended.

By the end of the stipulated term of these closed ended schemes, the debt portion of the fund grows to give you back the principal while the equity portion brings the potential upside. It is important to note that there are no guaranteed returns or guaranteed capital protection.

Tenures of these funds are mostly 1 year, 3 year or 5 years.

Example: SBI Capital Protection Oriented Fund – Series A (Plan 7)

launched on Jan 2020 with maturity after 1255 days (almost 3.4 years). Current allocation is 85.3% in debt, 9.7% in equity and rest in Cash & Equivalent.

73. CAPITAL PROTECTION FUNDS v/s CONSERVATIVE HYBRID FUNDS

Basis	Capital Protection Funds	Conservative Hybrid Funds
Objective	To protect principal and offer a potential equity-linked upside	To generate regular income and a potential equity linked upside
Type	Closed Ended – Pre-Defined Maturity	Open Ended
Invests in	Majorly in Debt of similar duration as their own term. Around 20% is invested in Equity as well.	Majorly in Debt (75-90%) and rest in Equity.
Risk	Medium Risk: As around 20% of investments in volatile Equity Instruments.	Medium Risk: Similar Equity risk as CPOFs but they carry higher Interest rate risks due to open ended nature of funds
Fund Management	Active	Active
Tenure	1, 3, and 5 years	N/A
Liquidity	Limited as you need to hold the fund till maturity. You can exit early by selling on stock exchange but the liquidity could be very low.	Very Liquid – You can redeem at any time but there could be Exit loads of up to 2% for redemption before 1 year.

Expense Ratio	Varies across plans and fund house but mostly few basis points higher than Conservative Hybrid Funds	Average expense ratio (Regular Plan) is 1.8%-2%
Taxation	Same as Debt Funds	Same as Debt Funds

Our Take:

We should avoid investing in CPOFs as being close ended funds, any performance data of these funds is not available and they also have little higher expense ratios due to higher marketing costs than Conservative Hybrid Funds.

74.   WHAT ARE FMPs?

Fixed Maturity Plans (FMPs) are close-ended debt funds. They are open for investment for a few days during NFO and then closed until pre-stated maturity. Maturity period may be just a month or as long as five years. FMPs invest in debt instruments such a money market instruments, bonds and government securities. Their fixed tenure often makes these comparable to fixed deposits.

The objective of FMPs is to provide steady returns over a fixed-maturity period, thus protecting investors from market fluctuations.

FMPs are passively managed, which means FMPs invest in debt instruments with the intent of holding them till maturity. So, a fund manager invests in instruments in such a way, that all of them mature around the same time. This means that regardless of any ups and downs in the market value of the investments, the final earnings are predictable. Therefore, the indicative returns FMPs provide to investors reflect the reality.

Generally, FMPs invest in high quality instruments, which have been rated by at least one credit rating agency.

Example: HDFC Fixed Maturity Plan - 1162 Days – March 2022

Launch date: March 15, 2022

Expense Ratio: 0.1%

Around 95% holdings in Government backed securities as of Dec 2022.

75. FMPs VS FIXED DEPOSITS

Basis	Fixed Deposits	FMPs
Returns	Assured returns indicated at the time of investing	Not assured. Returns are indicative in nature, based on the portfolio of securities bought. Though deviation from the indicative returns is mostly not significant.
Risk	Very Low as Banks rarely default and you also get insurance cover of upto ₹1 Lakh on your deposits	Little higher than FDs as there may be a likelihood of default by the company issuing the security. Mostly FMPs reduce this risk by investing in only highly rated (AA/AAA) funds.
Taxation	Returns from Fixed deposits are added to your income and taxed according to your tax slab	Gains from FMPs invested after 1st April 2023 are taxed as per your tax slab. Understand this better in *Q33*.
Liquidity	Fixed deposits score on liquidity as you can redeem earlier by paying some interest rate penalty (mostly 1%)	Only way you can exit from FMPs is by selling them on stock exchange but bear in mind that liquidity of FMP trade on Stock exchange is very low

Our Take:

Both FDs and FMPs are instruments for Conservative and Risk averse investors, who would like to invest money for a fixed tenure to meet certain financial goals in the future. Risk wise FDs score due to lower risk profile.

76. WHAT ARE REAL ESTATE MUTUAL FUNDS?

Real Estate Mutual Funds regulations were introduced by SEBI in 2008 under which these MFs could invest directly or indirectly in Real Estate assets. Regulations require that at least 35% of the portfolio should be held in physical assets. Securities that these funds can invest in include mortgage-backed securities and debt issuances of companies engaged in real estate projects. Not less than 75% of the net assets of the scheme shall be in physical assets and such securities. Assets held by the fund will be valued every 90 days by two valuers accredited by a credit rating agency. There were no takers of this regulation and no Asset Management company launched any scheme under this due to complicated regulation and audit requirement and lack of transparency in Real Estate sector in India.

Many Real Estate Private Equity Funds were launched in India under SEBI's AIF (Alternate Investment Fund) Regulations. These were closed ended funds with minimum 3 years lock in, where the key objective of the fund was capital appreciation. These funds invested in new residential or commercial projects and used to come out of it upon completion. The minimum investments allowed in these funds were ₹10 Lakhs, which was later increased to ₹1 Crore in May 2012 by SEBI. These investments are highly dependent on the performance of the builder in whose project the investments are made and on Real Estate market. So, these investments are meant only for high net worth individuals with high risk appetite. **Example**: HDFC Real Estate Fund, Kotak Realty Fund etc.

New type of fund called *Real Estate Investment Trust (REIT)* was introduced in 2014 budget. REITs are like mutual funds; they allow one to invest in income-generating real estate assets. The investment objective of REITs is to provide unit holders with dividends, usually generated from rental income and capital gains from the profitable sale of real estate assets. As on Dec 2022 there are only 5 REITs available for investment in India for Retail investors – **Embassy Office Parks REIT, Mindspace Business Parks REIT and Brookfield India Real Estate Trust.** Typically, the trust distributes 90 per cent of its income among its investors by issuing dividends.

Regulations for REITs require them to invest at least 80 per cent of their funds in completed, revenue-generating properties (majorly commercial properties). Only 20 per cent can be invested in under-construction property, listed shares of realty companies and fixed income instruments like gilts and money market securities. Till date no company has setup REIT in India due to tax and regulatory concerns, which all have been solved by Government and SEBI off late and therefore we are seeing many Global private equity companies and few Indian companies are now showing interest in setting up REITs in India. In next few months, we should expect few REIT listings.

There are no Mutual Funds in India which invest in Indian REITs as there are very few REITs. As REITs portfolio is expected to grow, we expect REIT specific Mutual Funds launches too in India. There are Mutual Funds which invest in International REITs like Kotak International REIT FoF.

Our Take:

You should avoid investing in Real Estate Mutual Funds (AIFs based) due to lockins and high risk and lack of transparency.

We believe REIT concept is a way forward for Indian investors and definitely the most promising way to invest in Real Estate till now. With Taxation benefit and setup of Real Estate Regulator, there is a lot to look forward to. You can consider taking some exposure in Real Estate through them.

77. WHAT ARE INTERNATIONAL OR GLOBAL FUNDS?

International Funds are Mutual Funds which invest in assets (Equity, Debt or other) listed outside India. Currently, there are more than 71 International Funds in Indian markets of different types. These funds are still not very popular but are gaining attention. These funds provide you with diversification opportunities outside domestic markets. Their taxation works like Debt Funds (Q33) irrespective of type.

Example: DSP US Flexible Equity Fund, Franklin Asia Equity Fund, etc.

78. TYPES OF INTERNATIONAL FUNDS PRESENT IN INDIAN MARKET?

Following are various types:

1. <u>Country Specific</u>: Most famous International Funds, these funds invest in equities of specific global countries. For **Example**:

    a. *Edelweiss Greater China Equity Offshore Fund*: A Fund of fund that will invest in companies domiciled in China or whose primary operations are in Greater China region.

    b. *Motilal Oswal NASDAQ 100 ETF*: An index fund which invests in NASDAQ 100 ETF. NASDAQ is a US based stock exchange.

    c. *HSBC Brazil Fund*: A fund of fund that invests in companies listed in Brazil.

2. <u>Region Specific</u>: These funds invest in assets listed in group of countries. For Example:

    a. *Franklin Asian Equity Fund: Principally invests in Asian companies/sectors, excluding Japan.*

   b. *Kotak Global Emerging Markets: Fund of fund that invests in mutual funds with a primary goal to invest in emerging markets.*

   c. *Edelweiss ASEAN Equity Off-shore Fund: An equity fund which invests primarily in companies of countries which are members of the Association of South East Asian Nations (ASEAN)*

3. <u>Commodity Funds</u>: These funds invest majority of their assets in global companies involved in commodity business such as mineral exploration, mining, agriculture etc. Few **Examples**:

   a. *DSP World Energy Fund: Invests in the equity securities of companies which have predominant economic activity in exploration, development, production and distribution of energy.*

   b. *ICICI Prudential Commodities Fund: Invests in commodities and related sectors.*

   c. *Aditya Birla Sun Life Commodity Equities Fund - Global Agri Plan : Invests in stocks of companies with principal business activity in or profiting from the agricultural industry.*

4. <u>Real Estate Funds</u>: These funds invest in assets of companies operating in Real Estate or Real Estate related sectors. They may also invest in global REITs. For Example: PGIM Ind Global Select Real Estate Securities FOF: Fund of funds which invests in stocks of companies operating in the real estate and real estate related sectors.

5. <u>Global Gold Funds</u>: These funds invest primarily in equity shares of companies involved in Gold Mining and extraction. Most of the times returns of these companies have a direct correlation with gold prices. **Example**: DSP

World Gold Fund: A fund of funds which invests mainly funds investing in gold mining stocks world-wide

6. <u>Hybrid</u>: There are few funds which invest majority of their assets (>65%) in domestic equity markets and some of it in international stocks. They are becoming popular as they are treated as normal Equity funds from tax perspective unlike full international funds and also give you some exposure to some high performing global stocks like Google, Apple etc. Example: Parag Parikh Flexicap Fund which has invested small amount of their assets in US companies such as Google, Amazon, Microsoft, Suzuki Motor Corp etc. and rest in Indian Equity stocks.

79. SHOULD I INVEST IN INTERNATIONAL FUNDS?

Pros and Cons

International funds surely give you additional diversification but do have some negatives as well. Let's understand the advantages and disadvantages:

Pros of International Funds

<u>Diversification</u>: International funds give you the diversification benefit of investing in global markets. If domestic markets are not performing well, then it is good to invest in global portfolios.

<u>Varied Options</u>: As we have seen in previous question, you have multiple themes and options to choose from.

<u>Adequate Track records</u>: Many of these are fund of funds that have invested in global funds which are very large funds with adequate track record to compare performance.

Cons of International Funds

<u>Currency Risk</u>: These funds face currency risk. Returns depend up on how the Indian currency is trading with the international

currency. If INR has depreciated, your returns would increase and vice-versa.

<u>Risk</u>: Overall risk profile for these funds is Very high as they are exposed to global market risk as well. The international governance plays a vital role in the performance of these funds and it gets difficult for Indian investors to comply with all policies.

<u>Taxation</u>: International funds are treated as Debt funds and taxed accordingly. So, gain on all the investments done on or after 1st April 2023 are taxed as per tax slab. Taxation is big negative for these funds for investors in high tax bracket.

Our Take:

International Funds are for seasoned investors who are looking for extra diversification in their portfolio. These types of funds are a good alternative for your or your child's foreign education goals as in that case, they help in overcoming currency risk and foreign country's inflation risk. Investments in these should be done by proper research and knowledge. These are high risk investments, which as per us should be avoided by amateur investors.

<u>Please Note</u>: As on 1st Feb 2023, there's an overall industry-level limit of $7 billion for mutual funds to invest in overseas securities and funds and a separate limit of $1 billion for investing in overseas exchange-traded funds (ETFs). Due to popularity of International Funds recently, these limits keep hitting max limit and hence many funds keep on restricting new investments in their funds. Before investing, do check if there are any investment restrictions on your fund. Industry has applied to RBI & SEBI to increase the limit since last 1 year but it hasn't been done yet.

80. WHAT ARE CHILDREN & RETIREMENT FUNDS? SHOULD I INVEST IN THEM FOR MY RESPECTIVE GOALS?

As per new categorization & rationalization of Mutual Funds as per SEBI's 06th Oct, 2017 circular, there came up a new category of mutual fund schemes called solution oriented mutual fund schemes. These schemes have been devised to provide solution to majorly two major life goals – Children Education & Retirement.

Features –

1. Lock-in: In case of retirement funds, there is a lock-in of minimum 5 years or retirement whichever is earlier. Similarly, in case of children education/gift funds, the lock-in will be 5 years or the child becoming a major (whichever is earlier).

2. Type of Investment: SEBI has not mandated any allocation benchmarks on these funds and fund houses can keep the allocation as per their wishes. We expect all of these funds to belong to either of these Hybrid categories – Conservative, Balanced Hybrid or Aggressive. To know more about these hybrid categories, please refer to Q45. Here are few examples -

    a. HDFC Retirement Savings Fund – Hybrid Debt Plan is a primarily a Conservative Hybrid Fund

    b. UTI Retirement Benefit Pension Fund is a Balanced Hybrid Fund.

    c. HDFC Children's Gift Fund is an Aggressive Hybrid Fund

3. Taxation: No special tax benefit. Same as other Hybrid Mutual Funds based on the allocation to Equity. Check Q44 for details.

Should I buy? – Mostly No, objectives such as saving for retirement or for children's education can be achieved equally, or perhaps more effectively, by investing in open-ended funds. Biggest issue with these solution oriented funds is their 5 year or more lock-in period and therefore in case the fund underperforms, investors cannot exit them and move their investments to a better-performing fund. They will have no option but to put up with the underperformance until the lock-in period ends. We believe, for your goals, you should opt for open ended Hybrid or Equity funds which gives you more options, much more flexibility and mostly better fund managers.

If we compare these funds with Insurance Children & Retirement Plans or NPS, these funds are much better in terms of returns, transparency and even taxation (w.r.t. NPS). These funds may also be suitable for investors who lack the discipline to stay invested in equities when the markets are passing through a bear phase. The lock-in will force them to stay invested, and not pull their money out at a loss.

CATEGORY 9

Systematic Transactions (SIP, STP, SWP)

81. WHAT IS SIP (SYSTEMATIC INVESTMENT PLAN)?

A Systematic Investment Plan or SIP is a mode of regular investments in mutual funds. SIP allows you to invest a certain pre-determined amount at a regular interval (weekly, monthly, quarterly, etc.). One of the best ways of entering equity market is through Systematic Investment Plans (SIPs) in equity mutual funds, as it brings in an investment discipline for your future cash flows and helps in Rupee cost averaging.

Few features of investment through SIP:

1. An SIP is a flexible and easy investment plan. Your money is auto-debited from your bank account and invested into a specific mutual fund scheme.

2. You are allocated certain number of units of Mutual Fund based on the ongoing market rate (called NAV or net asset value of the mutual fund) applicable for the day of SIP. Every time you invest money, additional units of the scheme are purchased at the market rate and added to your account. Hence, units are bought at different rates and investors benefit from Rupee-Cost Averaging, which means you get more units when market is low and less units when market is high and hence market averaging happens.

3. SIPs are done only in open-ended funds in which the investors can invest and take out the money anytime.

4. There is no fixed tenure for running an SIP. Even if you select an SIP tenure, if you wish you can stop it in between or you could continue it even after the tenure ends by placing a request with respective mutual fund company. You can also do a perpetual SIP.

5. Full and partial withdrawal is possible during or after the SIP tenure is over.

6. SIP amount can be increased or decreased.

7. SIP is an ideal tool of Mutual Fund investment for investors earning regular monthly income.

8. SIP is a method of investment in Mutual fund and hence its risk profile is equivalent to the type of asset you invest in.

82. WHY SHOULD I INVEST THROUGH SIP METHOD?

*   <u>SIP instils a habit of saving</u>- Half the work is done if you start a good habit. Through SIP an investor saves a part of his income first and then manages the expenses from what is left over. This habit of saving alone makes SIP method a winner among all.

*   <u>Reduces overall risk of investment</u>- With SIP, you avoid timing the stock market investment. You invest in each stage of market i.e. the highs and lows of the market, which results in steady capital appreciation.

*   <u>Power of Compounding</u>- SIP helps in an early start of investments as you can start small. Also, SIPs are mostly done for long term financial goals. These two factors of early start and long-term investment help you multiply your returns due to power of compounding.

*   <u>Convenience</u>- You can send an one-time instruction to your bank to allow auto debit of the investment amount each month from your savings bank account allowing systematic investments without worrying about missing out on any monthly investment.

Our Take

SIP is the best mode of investment in mutual funds due to all above reasons. It instils a saving and investment discipline in you. SIP is not a commitment but a discipline and this discipline alone can make you a successful investor.

83. WHAT IS STP? WHEN SHOULD I USE THIS FACILITY?

STP stands for systematic transfer plan. STP gives a facility to investor by which the investor can transfer a fixed or variable amount or units of funds from one scheme to another, at regular intervals (weekly, monthly or quarterly).

STP is majorly used to transfer money from debt funds scheme to Equity schemes. As during volatile markets, you may not feel confident to invest a lumpsum amount in Equities. So, in that case good strategy is to invest the lumpsum in Debt and start an STP to Equity, which spreads your investment in selected time frame. This is a good risk mitigation strategy.

As SIP is a good tool for people with regular income, STP from debt to equity funds can be utilised by people with lump sum income to systematically invest in equity market, if they are uncomfortable in investing a big amount in equity in one go.

An STP can also be used to transfer funds from an equity fund to debt, when a goal for which you have been investing for a long term has come within 3 years, when you would require the amount. This way you can protect your corpus from possible market fluctuation.

Key Features & Points to note

1. STP is a facility for convenience, when transfer happens from one mutual fund scheme to another it is still considered as selling units of the first scheme and then buying units in another one, so attract tax implications.

2. STPs can only be done from one scheme to other of the same fund house and hence, at initial investing stage, fund house should be selected based on the Equity scheme you want to invest in. For **example**: You cannot start an STP from HDFC Liquid fund to Axis Equity Fund,

but an STP from HDFC Liquid Fund to HDFC Equity fund can be done.

3. STPs can be done only among open ended Mutual Fund schemes.

4. Two types of STP:

   a. <u>Fixed STP</u>: In this only a fixed amount is transferred from one scheme to another

   b. <u>Capital Appreciation STP</u>: In Capital Appreciation STP, the investor takes only the profit part out of one fund and invests it in another. So, the amount is not fixed and depends on periodic profits.

84. WHAT IS SWP? WHEN SHOULD I USE THIS FACILITY?

SWP stands for systematic withdrawal plan. In principal, it is the reverse of SIP concept. In SIP, you look at accumulating a corpus by making regular investments into a mutual fund; in SWP, you regularly withdraw a fixed amount of money from your fund. Your fund's value and number of units will reduce to the extent of each withdrawal. The amount to be withdrawn and the frequency— monthly, quarterly, half yearly, or annually—are set by the investor.

For Example, Nilesh has 5000 units in a Mutual fund scheme and he wants to withdraw ₹4000 every month as SWP.

* On January 1, the NAV of the scheme is ₹10 hence 4000/10=400units will be redeemed in first month giving him ₹4000.

* At this stage, remaining units become 5000-400=4600.

* On February 1, let us say NAV of the scheme became ₹20, hence 4000/20=200 units will be redeemed in second month to him giving ₹4000.

* At this stage, remaining units become 4600-200=4400.

* This process can go on till all the units get exhausted.

Key Features & Points to note

* SWP is a method where you are assured of getting a fixed amount at your pre-determined frequency. The problem with other regular money options like monthly income plans, which pay dividends, is that the amount and the frequency of the payouts is not fixed.

* Withdrawals in SWP are treated as normal withdrawals. So, exit loads of the fund should be checked before starting an SWP.

* Since each withdrawal is essentially a sale of units, remember to check your tax implications on the redemption. You should start SWP only after remaining invested for at least a year in Equity funds and 3 years in Debt funds to reduce tax implications to the lowest.

* You cannot run an SIP and an SWP in the same fund.

* The number of withdrawals you can make from your fund corpus depends on the amount of withdrawal, size of your corpus and rate of the return of your fund.

* SWP should be used when:
  * You want a fixed periodic income in your retirement years, when you don't have any other income.
  * You are giving a fixed monthly expense to your child in hostel, out of his Education corpus.
  * You are planning for sabbatical leave and want to take care of you expenses from accumulated investments.

85. WHAT IS SWITCH IN MUTUAL FUNDS?

A switch in mutual funds is the transfer of funds from one mutual fund scheme to another in a single go. Switch can also be initiated based on few triggers set by an investor. **For example,** you can set a trigger that if Sensex touches 20000, switch X amount from your Equity fund to Debt fund.

Switch is basically selling units of one scheme and buying units of another scheme using the same amount. So please be aware about the exit loads and tax implications in case of switches. Switch can be done only between the schemes of same Mutual Fund house.

86. WHAT IS THE DIFFERENCE BETWEEN SIP AND LUMP SUM INVESTMENT?

We get this question very often but according to us it is not a fair comparison. SIP and lumpsum investment are two different methodologies of investment, one for an investor who has regular future income and another for an investor who has money at hand, respectively. So, putting it simply, if you have money at hand or have irregular income, you should do lumpsum investment and if you have a regular salary income, go for SIP. But things are always not so simple, so let's understand the difference between these two methods:

Basis	SIP	Lumpsum Investment
Mode of Investment	Investing the amount in systematic way i.e. investing a fixed amount periodically	Investing the amount at once in a Mutual Fund
Risk	Comparatively lesser risk as your investment gets spread over a period and hence absorbs some volatility of the market	Higher risk as markets can move either way post your investment
Key Benefit	Discipline: The biggest benefit of SIP is that it creates a discipline of saving and investment every month	Can time the market and can also transfer money systematically: If you think markets are at all time low, lumpsum investments can fetch you better returns. Also, if you think market is volatile, you still have an option of STP to enter the market systematically rather than through lumpsum investment.

Our Take:

Important it is to understand that the more time you give to an investment, higher would be the amount accumulated since the power of compounding increases as the time goes by. Understand the relation between the amount invested, the time invested and the rate of return earned. Giving your investment more time is wiser than taking undue risks by trying to time the market to earn few extra percentage point of return per year, which may not come out much in long term investments. So, whenever you have investible money, just invest!

87. SIP VS RECURRING DEPOSIT?

If you wish to invest small amounts of money on a regular basis each month, in the hope of gathering a large corpus after a few years' time, you may choose to go either the SIP (Systematic Investment Plan) or the RD (Recurring Deposits) route. Let's compare them:

Basis	SIP	RD
Investment	Through SIP, you may invest in Equity, Hybrid or debt Mutual Funds	Through RD, you invest in fixed deposit schemes of a bank
Frequency of Investment	You can do SIP with frequency daily, weekly, monthly or quarterly as per your choice	Frequency is mostly monthly
Returns	The returns obtained are dependent on the equity or debt market as per scheme chosen by the investor. Over the long run, better performing mutual funds have given double digit returns	Rate of return is fixed in RD and is known at the time of the start of RD account. Currently, RD interests are between 6.0%-7.5%.
Risk	Returns in SIP are variable and there can be a risk of returns and capital as per markets.	RD is considerably safe if deposited in an established bank.

Liquidity	You can stop the SIP anytime and redeem your investment subject to Exit load policy of the fund	With RD, premature withdrawal or closure will attract penalty charges
Taxation	SIPs, of course are more tax efficient as they invest in Mutual Funds. You should see *Q19, Q33* and *Q44* for more details	The interest earned on RDs is usually taxed as per one's income tax slab on accrual basis every year

Our Take:

SIP scores for long term investments due to better return profile and are also more tax efficient. We would suggest RD for short term goal saving (<2-3 years).

88. HOW SIP, STP & SWP TAXATION WORKS?

SIP - In the case of SIP every instalment is considered as a fresh investment. So if you have to get the benefit of long-term capital gains then each investment (SIP instalment) has to be held for atleast 12-month period in case of equity and for atleast 3 years in case of debt funds.

Example -Equity – SIP invested on 1st Apr, 2018 has to be held atleast till 31st March 2019 and an SIP invested on 1st May, 2018 has to be held atleast till 30th Apr, 2019 to get Long Term Capital Gain tax benefit.

Things are different in ELSS as there is a lock in of 3 years. So, each investment (SIP instalment) has a lock-in of 3 years. So, if you have done an SIP in an ELSS fund, each instalment will have its own 3 year lock-in. So, investment on 1st Apr, 2018 has to be held till 31st Mar 2021 and investment on 1st Mar, 2019 has to be held till 31st Mar 2022.

STP - When you transfer funds out of an equity or debt fund it will be treated as a sale and taxed accordingly. If you are transferring money out of debt/liquid funds into equity funds then any sale from debt/ liquid funds will be principal + capital gains and in that capital gains will be taxed as per your slab rate. On the other hand, if you transfer out of an equity fund then taxation of STCG & LTCG part will be taxed according to Equity taxation. You need to factor these tax implications and exit loads when deciding upon an STP. Example – Suppose you invested ₹2 Lakhs in HDFC Liquid Fund on 1st Apr, 2018. You have done an STP from HDFC Liquid Fund to HDFC Equity Fund of ₹10,000/month starting from 10th Apr, 2018. Then, in a Financial Year, total transfer is ₹1,20,000 (₹10,000 X 12). Suppose in this ₹1,20,000 – total gain is ₹8,000 and rest was principal. Then, since these gains are capital gains, these ₹8,000 gains will be taxed as per your income tax slab.

SWP - SWPs are normally done on debt funds or hybrid funds as their returns are more predictable compared to equity funds. In case of SWP, each withdrawal will be treated as a mix of principal and capital gains withdrawal and only the capital gains portion will be taxed. That makes an SWP a lot more tax efficient. Example – Suppose, you invested ₹6 Lakhs in Nippon India Short Term Fund on 1st Apr, 2015 and started an SWP of ₹10,000/month from it immediately from 10th Apr, 2015. So, this is how your taxation (Assuming you are in 30% tax bracket) will be –

Financial Year	Total Withdrawal	Principal	Capital Gain	Taxation
2015-16	₹1,20,000	₹ 1,11,000	₹9,000	30% of ₹9000
2016-17	₹1,20,000	₹1,04,000	₹16,000	30% of ₹16,000
2017-18	₹1,20,000	₹95,000	₹25,000	30% of ₹25,000
2018-19	₹1,20,000	₹80,000	₹40,000	20% of ₹40,000 (after indexation) – As investment was held for more than 3 years and invested before 1st April 2023.

These calculations are only illustrations. The capital gain and principal depend upon interest rates of that time.

89. WHICH IS THE BEST DATE FOR SIP IN MUTUAL FUNDS?

The day after you get your salary is the best day for your SIP. SIP is less of investing strategy more of a savings approach. There is no single 'best' day to run your SIP. Various theories are available, which may give preference towards different dates, but difference is minor and may not hold in future. So, it is important to invest as soon as possible.

90. RISK IN SIP INVESTMENTS? CAN THERE BE LOSS IN SIP?

SIP is an investment methodology where you invest in a Mutual Fund periodically. So, risk factors associated with SIP are same as that of the fund itself, irrespective of the way you invest. If SIP is started in an Equity Mutual Fund, then your investment would be prone to high risk, as the instrument is company shares and if you start an SIP in Debt fund, then it would be prone to low or medium risk as the instruments are Govt. Securities and Corporate Bonds etc.

We must know due to structure of SIP i.e. regular investments for long term, the market risk reduces by certain level as you invest in both ups and downs of the market. Therefore, you get returns which represents overall economy and market direction for the long term which is mostly positive. SIP is the best way to invest in volatile Equity markets.

Can there be negative returns from SIP? Of course, yes, there can be negative returns and there is higher chance in short term for equity funds. SIP returns in Equity are directly linked to stock markets and if they sustain consistent loses which can be a possibility in the short term due to volatile nature of the stock market, SIPs will also give negative returns.

SIP works on the principle of regular investments and brings the power of compounding to forth. It removes tensions and uncertainty from your investment plan by making it a mechanical regular process. It inculcates the habit of regular savings and does not encourage timing and speculation in the markets. But, remember that SIP is just another method of investing, it is a vehicle not the destination.

91. WHAT IS DIFFERENCE BETWEEN SIP VS FLEXI SIP VS VIP?

Basis	SIP	Flexi SIP	VIP
Amount Invested	Fixed every month	Variable and investor can choose different amount before every instalment	Variable and amount depends on the market performance in last month
Availability	All Fund houses	Some Fund Houses/ Online Brokers	Some Fund Houses/Online Brokers
Suitability	All type of investors	Investors with irregular income or seasoned investors who want pro-active approach	Not for all as amounts can vary a lot each month. Only seasoned investors should opt
Simplicity	Very simple to understand and execute	Little more complicated and needs your attention every month	Very complicated and you may not be able to guess the amount invested each month
Positives	Simple Predictable cashflows Lesser intervention No human emotions involved	Can invest more if you have irregular cashflows	Tend to give better returns as this approach invests more in bear markets and less in bull markets Scientific approach, no human emotions

Negatives	Fixed amount is invested even if markets are over-valued or undervalued	Manual intervention required every month Emotions can play a role Risk of lesser investment than required	Cashflows can be very erratic There could be months with no debit and other months where triple the regular amount is debited

Our Take:

Traditional SIPs are eternal.. You should avoid all these new innovations and stick to the good, old Traditional SIP investing. The real magic does not happen with these innovations, the real magic happens by investing through the ups and downs of the market and do that consistently over a long period of time.

92. WHAT IS STEP-UP SIP OR TOP-UP SIP?

In a Step-Up SIP, the amount of investment increases at a pre-defined rate and period. Since our salary mostly increases every year by a certain percentage, so it is wise to increase your SIP by same percentage every year. When you make an application for a fresh SIP, most fund houses ask you to specify whether you want to increase the investment amount periodically and by what amount.

For example, let us assume you started an SIP with ₹20,000, and you ask for a yearly top-up by ₹2000. So, after first year, your systematic investment will go up to ₹22,000 a month. Then, after another one year, it will go up to ₹24,000, and so on.

As our age increases, our income increases and it is obvious that our investments should also increase because our goals increase and the time horizon reduces. An SIP started at age of 25 at ₹10,000 may not be able to meet many of your financial goals, so it is important that you step up your SIP based on your average income growth each year.

So, we would suggest each investor to opt for Step Up/Top Up SIP option so that your salary increase can be put to good use pro-actively.

93. WHAT IS PERPETUAL SIP OPTION?

When you start an SIP, the mutual fund company or broker would ask you the start date and end date of your SIP. Instead of end date, most of the fund houses are giving option of Perpetual SIP which means SIP with no end date. It can only be stopped manually when required.

Few years back, this facility was not available and hence most SIPs would automatically stop after few months or years. Due to this stoppage, many a times paperwork needed to be done again to restart the SIP. More often than not, any sort of discontinuity interrupts the power of compounding. Therefore, we always would suggest you opt for Perpetual SIP and regularly review the performance. If you are not satisfied with fund's performance or your goals have reached, then you can always stop your SIP manually.

94. HOW ARE SIP RETURNS CALCULATED?

An SIP investment takes place on a particular date at regular intervals. When you make the investment, you will get a fixed number of units depending on the prevailing NAV of the scheme at that time. Over a period of time, you would accumulate a large number of units. That is why it becomes difficult to find out the total returns you have earned over a period. This is because every SIP instalment may have fared differently and have a different time period of investment. XIRR is a function in Excel for calculating internal rate of return or annualized yield for an array of cash flows occurring at regular / irregular intervals.

To calculate XIRR **what you need is:**

* SIP amount
* Dates of SIP investments
* Date of redemption (If you haven't redeemed the money but just want to check returns as of today, then put Today's date)
* Maturity (redemption) amount (If you haven't redeemed the money but just want to check returns as of today, then put Today's value of investment)

Illustration:

SIP of Rs 5,000 a month with redemption amount of Rs 31,000

Starting date of SIP: 01/01/2018,

Last SIP date: 01/06/2018

Redemption date of SIP: 01/07/2018

Then CAGR will be – 11.92%. Here is the calculation screenshot -

SIP Date	SIP Amount	
01/01/18	-₹5,000	
01/02/18	-₹5,000	
01/03/18	-₹5,000	
01/04/18	-₹5,000	
01/05/18	-₹5,000	
01/06/18	-₹5,000	
01/07/18	₹31,000	Redemption Amount
CAGR	=XIRR(E6:E12,D6:D12)	
	11.92%	

Where, E6 is first SIP amount,

E12 is Redemption amount,

D6 is first Investment date and

D12 is Redemption date, in the XIRR screenshot.

Websites/ Apps of mutual fund houses give you these calculations, when you enter the SIP amount, frequency, redemption date and scheme name.

CATEGORY 10

Investment Process in Mutual Funds

95. HOW SHOULD I SELECT AN EQUITY ORIENTED FUND?

Selecting the right equity fund is important as these are meant for the long term. Analysing qualitative and quantitative parameters can help you pick the right fund. Here are steps involved to do the same:

1. **Picking the right equity fund category:** Picking the right fund category is important before you turn towards qualitative and quantitative parameters. Equity funds are a good choice to achieve goals which are 5+ years away. Within pure equity funds these are three major types of categories:

    a) Large Cap funds – good for an investment duration of more than 5 years, which can give post tax returns of 11-12% p.a.

    b) Flexi cap/Multi Cap/Value/Focused Funds – good for an investment duration of more than 7 years which can give post tax returns of 12-14% p.a.

    c) Mid Cap Funds or Small Cap Funds – good for an investment duration of more than 10 years, which can give post tax returns of 12-15% p.a.

    For details on all categories of Equity Funds, please do refer to Q17.

    Above are ideal investment vehicles to achieve goals with said duration. But other aspects that impacts the category of fund you ultimately pick are, your financial position and your risk profile.

Financial position: You can achieve the same goal by selecting any of the categories defined above, but with each category the amount required to be invested will vary. Large cap funds would require a higher investment amount than mid cap funds to achieve the same goal. So, you could go for any category if you have the financial capacity to fund the amount. But if you don't have the capacity, you will have to pick a higher risk category to achieve your goal.

Risk Profile: You may not be very comfortable with higher risk involved with investing into small cap funds, but can have good night's sleep with stable large cap funds. So, based on this comfort level of yours, you could select a lower risk category, but remember the amount to be invested will be higher.

So, select an equity fund category based on the duration of investment, your financial position and your risk profile.

2. **Choosing the Right Schemes:** There are thousands of schemes to choose from. Once you have finalized the category, you should consider following factors to finalize the scheme:

    a) **Fund House pedigree:** You should be comfortable with pedigree of fund house – years in business, overall long-term performance of funds, their compliance record etc. This is not a criterion of selection but elimination. This criterion will help you remove few fund house schemes from further selection.

    b) **Historical Performance:** The most important criterion for selection of the scheme. You should choose the scheme which has a very good long-term record both against benchmark and peers. It is true that historical performance is no guarantee of future performance, but it gives a good pointer. We recommend you go for funds which have consistently outperformed their benchmark index and peers over medium-longer terms (3, 5 and 10 years). You should consider funds with minimum 7 years of historical performance and hence avoid new funds. Equity mutual funds are conducive for long term investments only. Thus, the focus should be on long term performance than a weekly, monthly or quarterly performance. It is important to check the **consistency** of the returns and not just trailing returns. While analyzing historical performance, focus more on Calendar and Rolling returns rather than trailing returns w.r.t. benchmark and category average.

1. **Trailing Returns:** Most popular way to represent Mutual Fund Returns. They are point to point returns and hence are highly influenced by recent performance of the fund. If today is 1st Feb 2023, then 1 Year trailing return means returns between 2nd Feb 2022 to 1st Feb 2023 and 3 year trailing returns means returns between 2nd Feb 2020 to 1st Feb 2023. Here are Trailing Returns of SBI Bluechip Fund as on 27th Jan 2023 (Screenshot from Fund-o-meter):

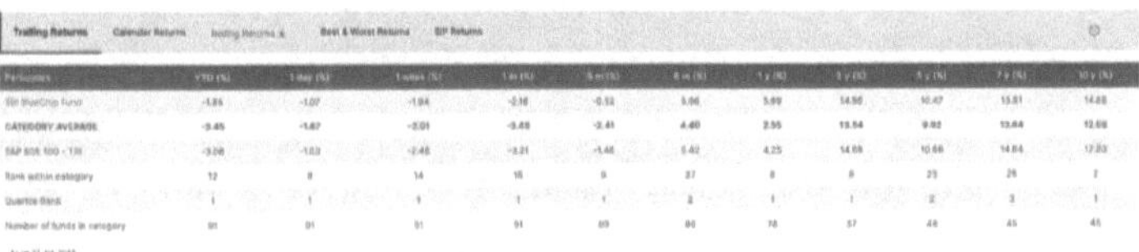

Trailing Returns   Calendar Returns   Rolling Returns &   Best & Worst Returns   SIP Returns

Parameters	YTD (%)	1 day (%)	1 week (%)	1 m (%)	3 m (%)	6 m (%)	1 y (%)	3 y (%)	5 y (%)	7 y (%)	10 y (%)
SBI Bluechip Fund	-1.86	-1.07	-1.94	-2.18	-0.52	5.06	5.99	14.96	10.47	13.81	14.88
CATEGORY AVERAGE	-3.45	-1.47	-2.01	-3.48	-2.41	4.40	2.95	13.54	9.92	13.44	12.69
S&P BSE 100 - TRI	-3.06	-1.03	-2.48	-3.21	-1.46	5.42	4.25	14.08	10.66	14.84	17.33
Rank within category	12	8	14	15	9	27	8	8	23	26	7
Quartile Rank	1	1	1	1	1	2	1	1	2	3	1
Number of funds in category	91	91	91	91	89	86	78	57	48	45	45

As on 27 Jan 2023

2. **Calendar Returns:** Calendar Returns means returns of the fund in a calendar year. You can check the consistency of the fund in beating benchmark and category average with these type of returns. Here are calendar returns of SBI Bluechip Fund which shows low consistency has fund has beaten both benchmark and category average only 3 times in last 7 years.

Scheme Name	2016 (%)	2017 (%)	2018 (%)	2019 (%)	2020 (%)	2021 (%)	2022 (%)
SBI Bluechip Fund	6.73	31.24	-2.68	12.13	17.17	28.50	6.11
Equity - Large Cap	5.94	31.70	1.68	11.23	14.92	28.09	3.76
S&P BSE 100 - TRI	4.89	33.27	2.27	10.62	16.70	28.09	6.02

3. **Rolling Returns:** Rolling returns are the annualized returns of the scheme taken for a specified period

(rolling returns period) on every day/week/ month and taken till the last day of the duration. Rolling returns have no recency bias like Trailing returns measures the fund's absolute and relative performance across all timescales, without bias. Here are Rolling Returns of SBI Bluechip Fund as on 31st Dec 2022. Clearly performance is very good in 7 years returns but not so much in 3 years.

RETURNS (Regular)

Trailing Returns	Calendar Returns	Rolling Returns	Best & Worst Returns	SIP Returns		
Particulars		3 Year Lowest (%)	3 Year Highest (%)	5 Year Lowest (%)	5 Year Highest (%)	7 Year Lowest (%)	7 Year Highest (%)
SBI BlueChip Fund		-3.95	29.05	0.95	21.71	9.12	16.17
Equity – Large Cap		-1.86	22.03	1.01	18.31	7.47	14.03
S&P BSE 100 – TRI		-2.85	21.13	0.78	18.75	7.18	14.71

As on 31 Dec 2022

c) **Fund Manager:** The credit for outperformance or underperformance of a mutual fund scheme lies with the fund manager (and his research team). You may not want to invest in a scheme with a new Fund manager. So, while selecting the scheme, you should look for the following info:

i. How long the current Fund Manager is working with the scheme and how has been the performance during his/her tenure

ii. How are the other schemes performing which are managed by this fund manager?

iii. If the fund manager is a new recruit, how has been his/her performance with past schemes

The fund houses which follow strict investment process and guidelines, new fund managers mostly cannot create too much flutter and therefore you should keenly observe the performance before taking any investment or redemption decision.

d) **Key Risk Ratios:** You and your advisor should also consider few ratios before selecting an Equity Fund scheme:

i. Alpha – Measure of how much the fund has outperformed its predicted return (Beta dependent). Look for higher alpha.

ii. Beta – Measures volatility. A beta of more than 1 (say 1.25) means that the fund is more volatile (25% in case of fund with Beta = 1.25) than the market. A lower beta indicates that the fund is more stable than the index.

iii. Sharpe Ratio – Measures returns (both positive and negative) with respect to risk taken. A good fund will get returns with the low amount risk and will have higher Sharpe Ratio.

iv. Standard Deviation: Standard Deviation measures how spread out the returns are from average returns. i.e. it measures the amount of variation of returns from its expected value. It is a statistical measure of risk. Larger the variability from expected value, bigger the value of standard deviation and higher is the inherent risk of investing in that scheme. Standard deviation is also useful for better understanding of returns. Looking at only the returns column of a scheme does not show you the full picture. For example, average returns may tell you that returns from an investment can be 10%, but in actual returns can be anywhere in the range from -5% to 25%, so that the average comes to 10%. Hence, standard deviation plays a major role in interpreting returns of a scheme and the risk involved in it. Lower the Standard Deviation, better it is.

e) **Other Factors** you should consider too but should not be your only criterion:

    i. **Asset Under Management:** Net assets of any scheme gives a fair idea of the confidence level of investors in the mutual fund scheme. Fund houses deploy their best fund managers for mutual fund schemes with high AUM. Therefore, this could be used as rejection criterion. You should reject the schemes with very low AUM as their volatility, expenses and risk profile could be higher. There is lot of debate that very high AUM Funds do not perform very well as due to high AUM, they diversify their portfolio more and also cannot invest in lower liquid stocks. With our research, yes High AUM funds are more diversified and hence take relatively lower risk but performances are mixed and there is no trend that high AUM funds do not perform as well as low AUM funds.

    ii. **Expense Ratio:** You should avoid schemes with very high Expense ratio. You should choose a scheme with average or below average expense ratio. Most of the established fund schemes will have lower expense ratio. Average Expense ratio of regular Equity funds (based on type) is between 1.8-2.2%. For direct Equity schemes, the expense ratio is around 0.5-1.2%.

    iii. **Exit Load:** There are few funds which charge very high Exit load as high as 3%. Though Equity fund investments are for long term but still you should avoid very high exit load funds as it kills your liquidity and ability to switch out in case of non-performance.

iv. **Fund Ratings:** There are many 3rd party agencies which give fund ratings such as investyadnya.in, Value Research, Morningstar and Crisil. You can refer to their ratings before finalizing the scheme to invest. Be aware that each agency has its own way of ranking mutual funds. But its a good confidence booster if your /your advisor's final shortlisted funds have good ratings on these portals.

v. **Portfolio Turnover:** A Portfolio Turnover Ratio represents the churn of the fund portfolio or the percentage of the portfolio holdings that have changed during the last year. Portfolio turnover is calculated by dividing either the total purchases or total sales, whichever is lower, by the average of the net assets. If a portfolio has a low turnover, it would mean that the fund follows a buy and hold strategy and that the fund manager has high conviction in picking his stocks. High portfolio turnover indicates high transactions and therefore higher trading costs, which ultimately impacts investor returns. Sometimes, a high turnover with high returns can be expected. However, a high turnover with lower returns is a red alert.

96. HOW SHOULD I SELECT A DEBT FUND?

Debt funds are meant for relatively short-duration investments—one month, six months, a year and so on upto a max. of 3 years. So, how do you decide which one is for you? Let's understand the steps:

1. **Investment Duration & Objective:** The first step in any debt fund investment is to determine your time horizon

(1 month, 6 months, a year etc.) and objective of the investment (Emergency Fund? Or Asset Allocation? Or Capital Protection? Or Regular Income? etc.)

2. **Finalize the Type of Debt Fund:** Based on your investment horizon, you should pick the type of Debt fund you should invest in. Biggest risk which you face in debt fund investments is interest rate risk and Credit Risk. For interest rate risk, the investment horizon of the fund and the calls that the fund manager takes on the direction and timing of interest rates will all have a bearing on your return. Therefore, you need to find a fund that has a time horizon that meets yours'. For Credit risk, to give extra returns, fund manager may take extra credit risk. To get the most out of your debt funds, match your investment horizon with that of the right type of debt fund. Please refer to *Q29* to understand all types of Debt Funds.

3. **Choosing the Right Schemes:** There are thousands of schemes to choose from. Once you have finalized the fund type, you should consider following factors to finalize which scheme suits you the most:

    a. **Fund House Reputation:** You should be comfortable with reputation of fund house – years in business, overall long term performance of funds, their compliance record, Total Debt Asset under management etc. We would recommend you select the fund houses who give higher or equal focus on Debt fund performance as Equity. This is not a criterion of selection but elimination. This criterion will help you remove few fund house schemes from further selection.

    b. **Historical Performance:** The not so important criterion for selection of the debt scheme. If a debt fund has performed too good w.r.t. category average, it mostly means the fund has taken higher credit risk w.r.t. category and hence is more risky. You should choose the scheme which performs near to category average, not too low and not too high too. It is true that historical performance is no guarantee of future performance, but it gives a good pointer. You can check Trailing Returns and calendar returns of the fund to check the consistency of the returns too. Avoid funds with very good performance w.r.t. category average.

c. **Credit Risk and Credit Rating –** A very important factor to select the Debt Fund as it helps you understand the credit risk the fund takes. Each debt instrument in India is mandatorily rated based on their credit worthiness by various credit rating agencies such as CRISIL, CARE and ICRA. Each rating denotes certain degree of risk involved -- for example AAA rating indicates highest credit rating. So, you can also assess the risk, fund manager is taking by checking the credit rating of the fund's portfolio. A large chunk in sovereign papers or highest rating papers implies that the fund is taking lower credit risk. Example: Here is the credit rating of ICICI Corporate Bond Fund as on 31st Dec 2022 which shows the fund takes low Credit risk as there is no paper with less than AAA rating:

Rating	Fund (%)	Category Average (%)
AAA/A1+	67.70	55.75
SOV	26.16	37.31
AA/A2	-	1.61
A & Below	-	-
Other	-	-

As on 31 Dec 2022

d. **Asset Under Management (AUM):** Net assets of any scheme gives fair idea of confidence level of investors in the mutual fund scheme. AUM is relatively an important criterion in Debt fund selection as almost 65% of total Asset under Management in Mutual Fund industry is in debt. Also, Fund houses deploy their best fund managers for mutual fund schemes with high AUM and also most of the high AUM funds take low risk too as lot of corporate money flows in Debt Funds and corporates do not want to take unnecessary risk with their money.

e. **Expense Ratio:** Much important selection parameter as compared to Equity Funds. High expense ratio can impact your Debt fund returns much more compared to Equity funds especially in low interest rate period. You should avoid schemes with very high Expense ratio. You should choose a scheme with average or below average expense ratio. Most of the established fund schemes will have lower expense ratio. Average Expense ratio of Debt funds (based on type) is between 0.3-1.7%

f. **Exit Load:** Since Debt funds are usually used to park money for short term, therefore it becomes more important to take care and avoid funds with high exit loads. Ultra-Short duration funds with any exit load, short duration funds with exit load after 180 days and medium & long duration funds with exit load after 365 days should be avoided.

g. **Key Ratios:** There are few parameters which can help you evaluate debt funds in better detail:

i. **Average Maturity:** The average maturity refers to weighted average time until all securities in a debt portfolio of a mutual fund mature. Lower the average maturity; the better it is in terms of the interest rate risk and lower volatility. So, liquid funds will have least Average Maturity (therefore safest) and Long-term gilt funds will have highest (therefore riskiest). You should match this average maturity with the duration of your investment.

ii. **Modified Duration (MD),** reflects the sensitivity of the debt securities' price when the interest rate scenario changes. It is based on the inverse relationship between the price of the bond and interest rates. This parameter helps in understanding the volatility of the fund. Lower the MD, lower the volatility. So, if modified duration is 6.4 years and the interest rate move up by 1% then the price of the security will move down by approx. 6.4%.

iii. **YTM (Yield to Maturity)** refers to the expected rate of return anticipated on a debt portfolio, if all instruments in the portfolio are held till maturity. So, if a Fund has YTM of 8.5% and Average Maturity of 4 years so it means the fund will give approx. 8.5% returns if you remain invested for atleast 4 years.

d. **Other Factors** you should consider too but should not be your only criterion:

    i. **Fund Ratings:** There are many 3rd party agencies which give fund ratings such as Fund-o-meter, Value Research, Morningstar and Crisil. You can refer to their ratings before finalizing the scheme to invest. Be aware that each agency has its own way of ranking mutual funds. But it's a good confidence booster if your /your advisor's final shortlisted funds have good ratings on these portals.

97. HOW SHOULD I SELECT A EQUITY ETF or INDEX FUND?

There are two steps to select the right ETF or Index Fund for you –

1. **Select the right Index** – This is the most important step. Here are 5 sub-steps which will help you in selecting the right Index for you –

    a. **Type of Index:** First you should know which type of Index you want to choose to invest. In Q59, we have discussed about all type of ETFs available in India.

        i. Broad Based Indices are diversified Indices and hence are most popular and least risky among the three categories. These indices have maximum AUM attached and also have high trade volume. Nifty 50 alone has about Rs 2.4L Cr AUM tagged to it as on Feb 2023. In these indices also, there are options to select Large Cap, Mid Cap and Small Cap broad based indices and therefore you should select the right one based on your risk profile and financial plan.

ii. **Sector/Thematic Indices:** Like Sector Funds, they are the most risky ETF/Index options. You should understand the sector and theme well before selecting this type of Indices type.

iii. **Strategic Indices:** In these type of Indices, index managing team put some algorithm over a broad based indices to generate extra alpha over them. They are relatively new and are gaining popularity recently. Some of these indices have created good alpha over broad based indices. They can be higher or lower risk compared to Broad based indices based on the strategy they are using. Example Low Volatility indices are generally lower risk than broad based indices whereas Momentum are higher risk.

b. **Know the options available:** Most of the domestic Indices are launched by either BSE or NSE in India. NSE Indices are more famous than BSE. Even though BSE and NSE have lot of indices but not all have respective ETF/Index Funds launched. Example: Nifty 200 is a popular Index and is a benchmark of many Mutual Funds and portfolios but there is no ETF or Index Fund launched through which we can invest in this Index. Hence it is important to know what Index options are available with us where we can invest. Here is the complete list of all Equity based Indices against which there is either an ETF or an Index Fund or both available to invest as on Feb 2023 -

Broad Based	Sector/Theme	Strategic
Nifty 50	Nifty Bank	Nifty 200 Momentum 30
Nifty Next 50	Nifty Private Bank	Nifty 100 Low Volatility 30
BSE Sensex	Nifty PSU Bank	Nifty Alpha Low - Volatility 30

BSE Bharat 22	Nifty IT	Nifty 50 Value 20
Nifty CPSE	Nifty Financial Services	Nifty Midcap 150 Quality 50
Nifty 100	Nifty Pharma	BSE Low Volatility
Nifty Midcap 150	Nifty 100 ESG Sector Leaders	Nifty Alpha 50
Nifty 50 Equal Weight	Nifty Auto	Nifty 200 Quality 30
Nifty Small Cap 250	Nifty Healthcare	Nifty Midcap 150 Momentum 50
Nifty 500	Nifty India Manufacturing	BSE Midcap Select
NIFTY 100 Equal Weight	NIFTY MNC	Nifty Dividend Opportunities 50
BSE 500	Nifty FMCG	BSE Enhanced Value
NIFTY Large Mid Cap 250	Nifty India Digital	Nifty 100 Quality 30
	Nifty India Consumption	NIFTY Growth Sectors 15
	Nifty Commodities	BSE Quality
	Nifty Financial Services Ex-Bank	
	Nifty Infrastructure	
	Nifty 50 Shariah	
	BSE Healthcare	
	BSE Financials ex Bank 30	

c. **Understand the Methodology:** Each Index has a different methodology and therefore different risk profile. Once you have created a shortlist based on above step (b), you should study the methodology of each Index in detail and should know how the stocks are selected in the index and how the rebalancing happens. Methodology documents are available on NSE & BSE websites. We have created detail videos on explaining methodologies of many of these index in detail on our Youtube channel Yadnya Investment Academy in our Mutual Fund Monday series.

d. **Historical Performance:** A very important criterion for selection of the right Index. You should choose the index which has a very good long-term record both against benchmark and peers. Avoid Indices (Not ETF or Index Funds) which are launched recently like many strategic Indices are launched recently and only their Back testing returns and not actual returns are available on NSE or BSE website. Go with Index which has atleast 7-10 years of historical performance (Doesn't matter even though funds or ETF tagged to them are launched recently). Equity Index funds/ETF are conducive for long term investments only. Thus, the focus should be on long term performance than a weekly, monthly or quarterly performance. It is important to check the consistency of the returns and not just trailing returns. While analyzing historical performance, focus more on Calendar and Rolling returns rather than trailing returns w.r.t. category average and other broad based index.

e. **Risk Ratios:** Like in Equity Mutual Funds (Q95), in selecting the right Equity ETF or Index Fund, risk ratios like Standard Deviation, Beta, Alpha and Sharpe Ratio would help you understand the risk profile of the ETF/ Index Fund w.r.t. a benchmark & category average. While calculating these risk ratios, it is import you select the right benchmark. Example: Nifty 50 Index can be compared to BSE Sensex or Nifty 100, Nifty 50 Equal Weight can be compared with Nifty 50 only. Strategic index can be compared with their underlying broad based index, example Nifty 100 Quality 30 can be compared with Nifty 100. Thematic Indices can be compared with BSE 500 or Nifty 500 to check their Risk profile.

2. **Selecting the right Index Fund Scheme or ETF Scheme:** Once you have selected your Index, next step is to select the right scheme as each Index may have multiple schemes to select. Example: There are about 36 ETF & Index Fund schemes which follow Nifty 50 Index. Here are few parameters to select the right scheme:

   a. **Expense Ratio:** Most important parameter to select the right scheme is the expense ratio. Lower the better since all the schemes are doing the same work i.e. to follow the index. **Example**: There are many ETFs with expense ratio of as low as 0.05% and among Index Funds, Navi Nifty 50 - Direct has lowest expense ratio of only 0.06% as on Feb 2023.

   b. **Tracking Error:** Tracking error is the divergence in the performance of the ETF/Index Scheme vis-à-vis the Index it is following. Tracking error arise due to some cash allocation with schemes may keep to manage investments and redemption, expense ratio and also due to inefficient investment process. Ideally the tracking error should be Zero but mostly it averages between 0.1% to 0.3%. High tracking error fund schemes should be avoided. You can get information about Tracking error on Fund Factsheet or on AMFI website at this link - https://www.amfiindia.com/research-information/other-data/tracking_errordata

   c. **Volume data & iNAV (only for ETFs):** In Index Funds, purchase & redemption are managed by fund house but in ETFs, purchase & redemption depends on liquidity of the ETF on the stock exchange. We have learnt about the difference in ETF & Index fund in detail in Q64. To understand if the ETF is liquid enough, it is important to know its trade volume on daily basis. Low Trade volume means it may be difficult for you to purchase or sell the ETF when it is required. Therefore always choose ETFs with high average trade volume. You can get the trade volume data of any ETF on NSE website.

While selecting an Index Fund or ETF, selecting the right suited Index is much more important than selecting the right scheme following it. Focus on first step more and second step is easy.

98. HOW SHOULD I SELECT HYBRID FUND?

Selecting the right Hybrid fund is combination of selecting the right Equity & Debt Fund. Based on the category, it is important to focus on both Equity and Debt parameters for analysis. Here are steps involved to do the same:

1. **Picking the right Hybrid fund category:** Picking the right fund category is important before you turn towards qualitative and quantitative parameters. Hybrid funds are a good choice to achieve goals which are 3-7 years away. Though there are various types of Hybrid Funds as discussed in Q45, we can divide them all in 3 major categories:

    a) Aggressive Hybrid Funds – Most popular category in hybrids with maximum Equity allocation. Good for high risk investors for horizon of 3-5 years. Expected returns: 10%-11%

    b) Conservative Hybrid Funds – Good for low risk investors for horizon of 3-5 years. Expected returns: 8%-9%

    c) Balanced Advantage, Multi-Asset, Equity Savings – Good for moderate risk investors for horizon of 3-7 years. Expected returns: 9%-11%.

It is very important that you choose the right category first to match your investment horizon and risk profile as the risk profile of each category in Hybrid is very different as equity allocation is very different in each category.

2. **Choosing the Right Schemes:** There are thousands of schemes to choose from. Once you have finalized the category, you should consider following factors to finalize the scheme:

    a) **Fund House pedigree:** You should be comfortable with pedigree of fund house – years in business, overall long-term performance of funds, their compliance record etc. This is not a criterion of selection but elimination. This criterion will help you remove few fund house schemes from further selection.

    b) **Historical Performance:** An important criterion w.r.t. to Hybrid Funds. You should give equal weightage to Historical Performance of the fund and the risk profile of the Hybrid Fund as in Hybrid, risk management is also very important. You should choose the scheme which has a very good long-term record both against benchmark and peers. You should consider funds with minimum 5 years of historical performance and hence avoid new funds. Thus, the focus should be on long term performance than a weekly, monthly or quarterly performance. It is important to check the consistency of the returns and not just trailing returns. While analyzing historical performance, focus more on Calendar and Rolling returns rather than trailing returns w.r.t. benchmark and category average. You can get details of these type of returns in Q95.

c) **Fund Manager:** Most of the Hybrid Fund managers have multiple fund managers, separate fund manager for Equity allocation and separate for Debt allocation. It is important that we give weightage to both fund managers as Debt risk management in Hybrid is also very important esp. in Conservative or Balanced Adv type of categories. So, while selecting the scheme, you should look for the following info:

   i. How long the current Fund Manager is working with the scheme and how has been the performance during his/her tenure

   ii. How are the other schemes performing which are managed by this fund manager?

   iii. If the fund manager is a new recruit, how has been his/her performance with past schemes

The fund houses which follow strict investment process and guidelines, new fund managers mostly cannot create too much flutter and therefore you should keenly observe the performance before taking any investment or redemption decision.

d) **Key Risk Ratios:** You and your advisor should also consider few ratios for both Equity & Debt

   i. Equity/overall Risk profile – Like we have discussed in Equity Funds selection (Q95), we should review the hybrid funds too on Risk parameters such as Standard Deviation, Beta, Alpha, Sharpe Ratio etc. to understand the overall risk profile of the fund w.r.t. benchmark and category average

    ii.   Debt – Like we have discussed in Debt Funds selection (Q96), we should measure the risk profile of the debt portfolio of the hybrid fund through Credit Rating, Average Maturity, Modified Duration and YTM.

e)   **Other Factors** you should consider too but should not be your only criterion:

    i.   **Expense Ratio:** Hybrid Funds has higher expense ratio than Debt funds and equivalent to Equity funds as the fund manager managerial involvement is more and there are no ETF/Index funds in the competition too. You should avoid schemes with very high Expense ratio. You should choose a scheme with average or below average expense ratio. Most of the established fund schemes will have lower expense ratio. Average Expense ratio of Hybrid funds (based on type) is between 1.4-2.2%. For direct Equity schemes, the expense ratio is around 0.7-1.2%.

    ii.   **Fund Ratings:** There are many 3rd party agencies which give fund ratings such as investyadnya.in, Value Research, Morningstar and Crisil. You can refer to their ratings before finalizing the scheme to invest. Be aware that each agency has its own way of ranking mutual funds. But its a good confidence booster if your /your advisor's final shortlisted funds have good ratings on these portals.

99. HOW TO REVIEW YOUR MUTUAL FUNDS PORTFOLIO?

Your mutual fund portfolio should be reviewed atleast once in a year. Following should be the objective of your review:

* **Performance of Fund:** You should not just check standalone performance of a fund. Performance is a relative issue. Always compare:

    a. **Fund Scheme vs Benchmark:** Compare your fund with benchmark. Main objective of the actively managed funds is to beat the benchmark and they should be able to do it consistently.

    b. **Fund Scheme vs Category/Peers:** Comparing fund with benchmark may not be enough as beating benchmarks is fairly easy for Indian fund managers. So, it is important to compare fund performance with its top performing peers or overall category.

* **Asset Allocation:** If you have any fixed asset allocation in mind for your portfolio, you should review it atleast once a year and make changes accordingly. Please keep in mind tax implications while making changes.

* **Changes in Fund Scheme:** You should be aware about the major changes happening in a fund you have invested in, such as change in scheme's investment objective, change in fund manager or any acquisition or merger of fund house etc. If any such major event has happened, you should review that particular scheme more often to see if there is any impact on performance. If your fund is under performing consistently after such a change, you should find out the exact reason for this and take a call whether to switch your funds.

* **Goals or Goal Post changes:** If your goals have changed or current goals timelines have changed or if your goals are nearing their investment horizon, you should make changes in your portfolio accordingly. **Example:**

a. If you have decided to go for a foreign vacation next year with family, then you will need to put your extra savings in debt funds.

b. A goal like child's higher education for which you have been investing in equity since a long time, is within 3 years now, see when you should start moving the corpus to debt instruments, to keep the corpus safe.

Our Take:

Your entire portfolio should be at least 5 Years old, to carry any significant changes due to pointers listed above. We suggest young investors to review the patterns and monitor the portfolio but do not make too many fund changes too soon. Short term bad performance of a fund doesn't mean it is a bad choice.

100. WHEN SHOULD I SELL MY MUTUAL FUND?

Following are **typical reasons when people think they should sell their Mutual Funds**:

1. Market is at all time high and your funds have performed much better than expectations. You are looking to book profits by selling them.

2. Markets are not performing, and your funds have given negative returns. You are thinking to move out of equity to reduce further losses.

3. Fund is performing below peers. Many a times for few months, funds may underperform making us think our fund is not good enough.

If any of the above reason is making you think about selling your fund, then such sell decisions mostly backfire. Following should be the **only reasons** when you should consider selling your mutual fund:

* **You have achieved your goal:** The ideal time to sell your MF holdings is when your financial goals are very near of completion, may be few months before. If you have invested in an equity fund, you should shift your investments to a low risk debt fund 1 to 3 years before reaching your goal to save yourself from volatility of equity markets in the ending years.

* **Scheme underperformance for long term:** If the scheme you have invested in is underperforming consistently for long time (4-6 Qtrs.) relative to its benchmark and peers, then you should try to understand the reason for underperformance, like is it because of change in Fund manager, change in fundamental attributes or any other structural changes and accordingly take a call to switch the fund.

* **Re-balancing due to change in your Risk profile:** If with increasing age, changing salary, expenses and goals there is a possibility that your risk profile may change. **Example**: If you are now in middle age, your risk profile may become aggressive from highly aggressive. In such case, if your financial status allows, you may want to sell some of your equity funds to move to Debt.

Our Take:

You should stay invested for a longer term, unless there is something really wrong with the fund or you need liquidity.

101. WHAT SHOULD I DO IF MY MUTUAL FUND HOUSE IS ACQUIRED BY OTHER FUND HOUSE OR THERE IS OTHER MAJOR CHANGE AT AMC LEVEL?

Mergers and Acquisitions are very common in Mutual Fund Industry. Recent examples – L&T MF was acquired by HSBC, Blackrock leaving DSP, IDFC MF acquired by Bandhan consortium, Quant buying Escorts MF, Baroda MF and BNP Paribas MF merged. Merger & Acquisition does impact investors as there is change in management and probable change in Fund's objective too.

Whenever there is a change in the fundamental attributes of a scheme (Post M&A), investors have to be given notice of the proposed change and the option to exit the scheme at the prevailing NAV without paying exit loads. Please remember, investor will still have to pay capital gain tax on this exit.

What should investor too? Investors should review the change from multiple angle:

1. <u>Change in Scheme objective</u>: Post M&A, has the scheme objective of the fund you have invested changed? **Example**- post merger of Baroda and BNP Paribas, Baroda Hybrid Fund was changed from an aggressive Hybrid Fund to Balanced Advantage Fund. This is a major change and if you think this changed doesn't suit your profile, you should exit the fund.

2. <u>Change in Fund Management Team</u>: You should review if post M&A, has the fund management team changed too? If yes, then you should definitely put it under close review and see how is new management team and accordingly take action.

3. <u>Past Performance of new Management</u>: If a known Fund house has acquired your fund, for example HSBC MF acquired L&T MF, then you should check the earlier performance of acquirer and if you are comfortable then you should continue, if not you can exit or give some time to new management

4. <u>Under-performance for few months should be considered</u>: M&As are big event for fund houses and lot of internal processes get changed and lot of uncertainty

is there for old management team too. In such situation, under-performance for few quarters should be considered and avoid panic action.

102. HOW TO INVEST IN MUTUAL FUND?

To start Mutual Fund investment, you need a PAN, a Bank account and be KYC (Know your Customer) compliant. If you are not sure about your KYC status, you should check at any of following websites of KYC registration agencies by entering your PAN.

* www.cvlkra.com
* camskra.com
* www.karvykra.com
* kra.ndml.in
* www.nsekra.com

The need for KYC is to comply with the SEBI's regulation in accordance with the Prevention of Money laundering Act, 2002 ('PMLA'). If your KYC is not done, you need to get it done at any place you choose to invest through, in Mutual Funds by submitting following documents

* Filled KYC form
* Recent passport size photograph
* Self-attested PAN Card copy
* Self-attested Proof of address copy

Remember, KYC is just a one-time process and once done, you can invest in any mutual fund scheme through any below mentioned way.

Like, many mutual fund schemes to choose from, there are several ways in which one can invest in them. There are both online and offline methods and each has its own pros and cons. Let's discuss:

1. **Directly with the Fund house:** You can go to any fund house office and open your mutual fund account. Account can be opened online as well if your KYC is done.

   Pro: You can invest in Direct plans as well. Details about Direct plans is in Q108.

   Cons: a) Can only invest in one Fund house's schemes. B) Selecting the fund house and doing all the paperwork yourself can be tough.

2. **Through distributors/IFAs (Independent Financial Advisors):** You can also invest through AMFI registered distributors who can give you basic Mutual Fund advise, explain all the Mutual Fund jargons, and can help you in doing all the paperwork as well as sending reports etc.

   Pros: a) You get basic advice and can ask your Mutual Fund related questions. B) No paperwork headache, IFAs help you with that. C) Tracking your investments and suggesting the changes

   Cons: a) You cannot invest in Direct Plans. B) Risk of biasness based on their commission through each fund scheme.

3. **Through RIA (Registered Investment Advisors):** RIA are investment advisors registered with SEBI. They act on fiduciary capacity. They do not get any commission from Mutual Fund and would have you invest in direct plans but do charge a fixed or variable fee for their advice.

   Pros: a) They can act as complete financial advisors for you with knowledge outside Mutual Funds as well. B) Can invest in Direct plans c) Can help you with paperwork and help you track and review your investment. D) Unbiased advice.

   Cons: a) You should be very clear on their fees structure. B) You need to issue them separate cheques for their services as they do not get any money as commission.

4. **Through CAMS/Karvy or MFCentral:** CAMS and Karvy are R&T agents of Mutual Funds and gives free online access to many AMC's schemes. Individuals can go to CAMS/Karvy office to open their Mutual Fund account and KYC registered customer can do it online as well through their website. MFCentral is a mutual fund transaction platform brought about by CAMS and Kfintech (i.e. Karvy). MFCentral brings about the convenience of services like change in bank details, nominee details, contact number, email id, etc. You can view your combined MF portfolio here (PAN and mobile number based) and also execute your MF transactions.

    Pros: a) Completely Free online access to all major AMC schemes (to all AMC schemes in case of MFCentral). B) Can invest in direct plans as well c) Mobile apps and consolidated info gives convenience d) Even RIAs and distributors use these platforms to give you online access to your portfolio.

    Cons: These platforms do not give any advice or goal planning, etc. and you will have to depend on your advisor or do it yourself.

5. **Through your Bank:** Most of the banks also act as Mutual Fund distributors. So, you can approach your bank to open a Mutual Fund account as well which can be easily integrated with your online banking account.

    Pros: a) Banks have relationship managers who have sound knowledge of financial industry. B) Convenience of managing your mutual fund account through your online banking is great. C) Convenience of nearby bank branch for any query or changes or advice or cheque submission etc.

    Cons: a) You cannot invest in direct plans through them b) Risk of not getting an unbiased advice

6. **Through many Robo-advisory Portals:** Today, there are a number of online robo-advisory portals, which gives

you online financial advice, execute your mutual fund transactions and few also give you access to a on call financial expert. There are number of new business models available and many coming up in this space. Few worth mentioning- Groww, Paytm Money, FundsIndia, Zerodha Coin etc.

Pros: a) These portals have a great User interface b) Biggest benefit is easy and low cost advise given by these portals c) Value added services such as creating financial plan, tax planning, insurance planning etc. d) Excellent analysis and reports on your portfolio.

Cons: a) Minimal human intervention can make you understandably apprehensive about the advice b) Too many options available in the market make the choice very complicated and once stuck, it is difficult to come out of it c) These portals tend to do information overload which might be overwhelming for amateur investors. d) May charge fees in the future or may try to sell you their other high commission products.

103. WHERE CAN I LOOK FOR INFORMATION ON MUTUAL FUNDS?

There is a lot of information on the web where you can know about Mutual Fund markets, schemes and news. Following are few good ones:

1. **SEBI website:** SEBI website has info on all the Mutual Fund regulations and all the latest NFO's offer documents. There is also a lot of educational material in their investor education section.

2. **Mutual Fund house's website:** Most of the fund houses have all the latest and extensive information about their own fund schemes: Daily NAVs, latest news, Scheme

information documents, Monthly factsheet, investment forms and online transaction option.

3. **AMFI website:** All the latest information about Mutual Fund schemes and industry numbers: Daily NAV, AUM data, NFO info, distributor info, all historical data etc.

4. **Other websites:** There are many third-party websites, which give useful analysis, comparison, news and rating on mutual fund industry. Few worth mentioning are:

    a) investyadnya.in/fundometer

    b) Moneycontrol.com

    c) ValueResearchonline.com

    d) Crisil

    e) Economic Times

    f) Morningstar.in

CATEGORY 11

Mutual Funds Operations

"An investment operation is one which, upon thorough analysis, promises safety of principal and an adequate return. Operations not meeting these requirements are speculative."

–Benjamin Graham

104. WHAT IS THE STRUCTURE OF MUTUAL FUND?

A mutual fund is setup in a form of a trust, which has sponsor, trustees, asset management company and a custodian. It is regulated by SEBI and follows the guidelines of AMFI (Association of Mutual Funds in India).

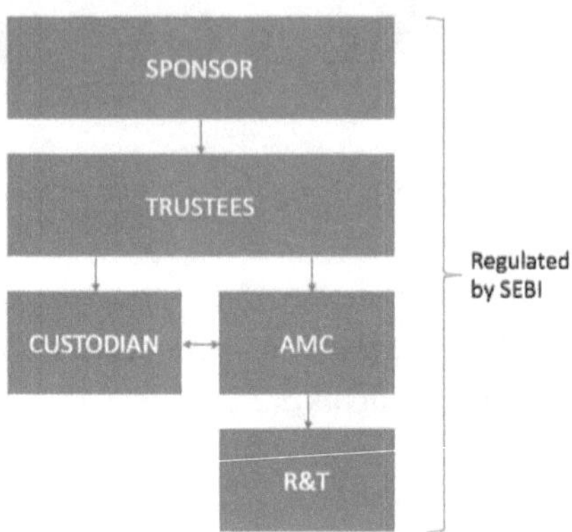

1. **Sponsors:** Sponsors establish the trust; they are like the promoters of any company. The responsibility of the sponsor includes appointing the trustees with the approval of SEBI and setting up an AMC. Example: ICICI Bank and Prudential Plc are sponsors for ICICI Mutual Fund.

2. **Trustees:** Board of Trustees/ board of directors who track the performance and maintain the compliance with the rules stipulated by SEBI. They ensure the interest of the unit holders is protected. At least two thirds of the trustees or the directors should be independent not associated with the sponsor in any way. Example: ICICI Prudential Trust Limited is the company which acts as Trustee for ICICI Mutual Fund.

3. **Asset Management Company (AMC):** AMC or Mutual Fund house is the company responsible to manage the

assets of the Mutual Funds and takes care of its day to day operation. The AMC consists of the Chief Investment Officer, the fund managers and analysts, who are together responsible for managing the various schemes launched. ICICI Prudential Asset Management Company Ltd is the AMC of ICICI Mutual Fund.

4. **Custodian:** Custodian is registered with SEBI and has the custody of the all the shares and various other securities bought by the AMC. The custodian is responsible for the safe keeping of all the securities. HDFC Bank is the Custodian of ICICI Prudential Mutual Fund.

5. **Registrar & Transfer Agents:** The AMC appoints the registrar and transfer agent to the mutual fund. The registrar processes the application form, redemption requests and dispatches account statements to the unit holders. The registrar and transfer agent also handle communication with investors and updates investor records. There are only two Registrar in the industry currently – CAMS & Karvy. By volume, CAMS has about 70% market share in managing MF transactions. Here is the list of Mutual Funds serviced by CAMS and Karvy respectively –

AMC Serviced	
CAMS	**Karvy**
ICICI Pru	Axis
HDFC	Canara Robeco
Aditya Birla SL	Edelweiss
DSP	IDBI
Franklin Templeton	Invesco
HSBC	LIC

IDFC	Mirae Asset
Kotak	Nippon
PPFAS	Navi
SBI	Quant
Tata	Quantum
Union	Sundaram
Whiteoak	UTI
Shriram	Trust
Mahindra	Taurus
IIFL	Samco
	PGIM
	Motilal Oswal
	JM Financial
	NJ
	Baroda BNP Paribas
	Indiabulls
	Bank of India

6. **Regulator:** The Securities and Exchange Board of India (SEBI) is the primary regulator of mutual funds in India. SEBI's Regulations called the SEBI (Mutual Funds) Regulations, 1996, along with amendments made from time to time, govern the setting up a mutual fund and its structure, launching a scheme, creating and managing the portfolio, investor protection, investor services and roles and responsibilities of the constituents.

The Association of Mutual Funds in India (AMFI) is the Industry body that oversees the functioning of the industry and recommends best practices to be followed by the industry members. It also represents the industry's requirements to the regulator, government and other stakeholders.

105. WHAT IS THE ROLE OF A FUND MANAGER?

Manager's roles & responsibilities

Fund managers are professionals in the fields of Financial Analysis & wealth management, who are responsible for managing investors' money to achieve the scheme goals. Star fund managers are in a lot of demand in the industry and they attract more investments due to their performance.

Role & Responsibilities	Brief Description
Stock Picker/ Portfolio Builder	In charge of what stocks, bonds or other assets the fund buys with investors' money
Asset Allocation	Decides how much cash has to be carried and the proportion of assets in various categories
Portfolio Strategy	Decides whether to adopt Top Down or Bottom Up approach, etc. Whether to go for Growth or Value Stocks
Sector Exposure	Bet on a certain sector. Take over/ under exposure to a certain sector.
Reporting & Compliance	Make sure regulatory reporting requirements and ethical standards are met
Wealth Protection	Follow risk management techniques, right diversification
Discussion with Company's top Management	Know and discuss Short Term and Long term plans of companies you are invested or plan to invest
Meeting Institutional Investors	Keep big investors informed and attract more funds

Communicate with Retail Investors	Analysing major market events
Hiring, Outsourcing and Oversight	Hire, oversee staff and outsource certain duties

106. WHAT IS EXPENSE RATIO OR TOTAL EXPENSE RATIO (TER)?

To manage your money, a mutual fund house/AMC incurs some expenses such as fund management fee, agent commissions, registrar fees, auditor fees, advertising expenses, etc. To manage these expenses, fund house charge a fee for their services which is called Expense Ratio. Expense ratio states how much you pay a fund in percentage terms every year to manage your money.

Example: If you invest ₹20,000 in a fund that has an expense ratio of 2%, you have to pay ₹400 for managing your money. So basically, if a fund earns 10% and has a 2% expense ratio, it would mean an 8% return for you. Now, this example has been given just for explanation purpose. In reality, all the returns and NAV we see on various Mutual fund websites mentioned in *Q103* are expense ratio adjusted. So those are the return values which you will actually get when you redeem them and you do not need to reduce TER from it.

SEBI has stipulated a maximum limit on these Expense ratios. Equity funds can charge maximum upto 2.5%, debt funds can charge max upto 2.25% & index funds can charge max upto 1.5% of average weekly net assets. Always remember, irrespective of whether a fund generates positive or negative returns expenses are always incurred.

SEBI guidelines further set sub-limits for TER based on the size of the assets managed. For equity schemes, fund houses can charge 2.5% for the first ₹100 crore, 2.25% for ₹100 crore to ₹400 crore, 2% on the next ₹400 crore to ₹700 crore and 1.75% on any sums above ₹700 crore.

For debt schemes, the limits are 25 basis points lower in each slabs. An additional 30 basis points can be charged by the mutual fund if 30 per cent or more of their inflows are received from beyond the top 30 cities.

Also, a lower expense ratio does not always mean that it is a better-managed fund or will give better returns. A good fund is one that delivers good return with minimal expenses. A lower or higher expense ratio does not make a fund good or bad. It also does not matter when there is a good amount of difference in returns of funds you are comparing. It matters where two funds look almost similar in almost all aspects, but have a sizable difference in their expense ratios.

107. WHAT ARE MUTUAL FUND LOADS?

Apart from TER, there are few one-time charges too, which are levied. These are called loads which are levied either at the time of investing in or at the time of exiting a mutual fund scheme. These are over and above the TER.

1. **Entry load:** It was a charge which was levied at the time of investment in Mutual Funds. But SEBI abolished entry loads in 2009. So currently, there is NO Entry load on all Mutual Fund Schemes.

2. **Transaction charge:** From 2011, SEBI has allowed AMCs to collect a nominal amount as a one-time transaction fee, called transaction charge. Following are the details:

Particulars	Investment Amount	Fees Payable
First Time Investor	Less than ₹10,000	Nil
	More than ₹10,000	₹ 150
Existing Investor	Less than ₹10,000	Nil
	More than ₹10,000	₹ 100

In case of SIPs, where your total SIP outgo is more than ₹10,000, a transaction charge of ₹100 will be applicable, deducted in four consecutive equal instalments starting with your second instalment.

3. **Exit Load:** These are the charges which are liable to be paid in case an investor exits a fund before a specified time frame. Mutual funds charge exit loads to discourage investors from leaving mutual fund schemes within a short period. Liquid Funds do not charge any exit load as they are meant for short term only. Every fund defines its own exit load, mostly in the range of 0.25% to up to 3% depending on the type. A fund can either have one exit load – like 1% on redemption before 365 days, Or, it can adopt a staggered approach, charging 1.5% for redemptions before 365 days, 1% on redemption between 366 and 730 days, and 0.5% on redemption between 731 and 1095 days.

108. WHAT ARE DIRECT PLANS IN MUTUAL FUNDS?

Direct plan schemes are schemes in which you invest directly with a Mutual Fund house. In such plans, there are no intermediaries or distributors or brokers involved and therefore expense ratio of these plans are lower than the regular ones as AMC saves on distribution cost. Thus, saving 0.2- 1% in expense ratio. Direct plans were introduced by SEBI in Jan 2013 to give options to corporate and experienced mutual fund investors to reduce their expense ratio. They have already become popular with more than 1/3rd of investment already done through direct route.

You will get to invest through direct plans only, if you invest directly through mutual fund office, website or their R&T agents such as CAMS & Karvy. Recently, there are few online portals (such as Paytm Money, Groww, Upstocks, Zerodha Coin etc) started too, which invest your money only in Direct plans, they may charge a fixed yearly fees.

However, remember the investment objective, investment mix and everything else except expense ratio & NAV of the scheme portfolio would be same as regular plans. The scheme would denote "Direct" in its description at the end of such direct plans.

Example: This is how you will see the name of direct and regular plans when you will invest:

Mirae Assets Emerging Bluechip Fund–- Direct Plan (Expense Ratio – 0.68% as of Dec 22)

Mirae Assets Emerging Bluechip Fund – Regular Plan (Expense Ratio – 1.7% as of Dec 22)

109. DIRECT OR REGULAR PLAN, WHICH ONE IS FOR ME?

Under regular plans, you invest through a distributor or an intermediary, whereas in direct plans you invest directly with AMC. Thus, cost (expense ratio) is higher for regular plans. Remember you do not pay anything directly to the distributor or any intermediary, AMC does and that results in higher cost i.e. expense ratio.

Which on you should choose? Direct plans seem to be a natural answer, as it will give always give higher returns than the regular plan which when compounded becomes a good amount after few years. However, the answer is not so simple. It is same as taking a self- medication and not consulting a doctor or filing your tax returns of your own to save CA cost. It may work for some and can have adverse impact for others.

Ideally, direct plans suit corporate customers who can hire their own advisor and save distributor cost and for knowledgeable and disciplined investors who can do their own research before investments, track and review their portfolio regularly and make changes and are disciplined enough to keep investing and stay invested without being affected by daily market fluctuations.

For others, a good financial advisor brings a lot of benefits on the table such as selecting the right scheme for you, helping with all paperwork, tracking the performance and making changes, keeping you disciplined in investment, saving you from making impulsive decisions during market cycles, etc. and if they are doing all this, they deserve to be compensated too. Ultimately, what you need to think about is the choice of going direct in context to your ability to service that investment and make the right decisions. Making just the wrong choice of scheme can wipe out the benefit or even more by going direct.

110. WHAT IS A MUTUAL FUND BENCHMARK?

Benchmark is the reference point with which Mutual Fund scheme's performance is compared. Since 2012, SEBI made it mandatory for fund houses to declare a benchmark index for each of their schemes. Benchmark is something your fund mostly correlates to. These benchmarks are usually a well-established index of securities. It is mandatory for fund houses to show scheme performance against the benchmark while marketing a scheme.

The whole point of investing in a large cap mutual fund is that it should give you better returns than these indices, otherwise you can always invest directly in these indices (through index funds) and get the same returns with much lesser expense ratio.

From 1st Jan, 2022, SEBI has introduced two tier benchmarking structure for Mutual Funds. The Tier 1 benchmark will indicate the scheme's category, and the Tier 2 benchmark will indicate its specific investment strategy. The markets regulator's intent behind circulating a standardised approach in benchmarks is to bring uniformity across mutual fund schemes. Tier 1 benchmark are compulsory and are published by AMFI (Association of Mutual Funds in India) based on which each scheme of the category has to keep that as primary benchmark. Tier 2 benchmark will be optional. The Tier 2 benchmark must be finalised by the AMCs as per the investment strategy of the scheme or its style. **Example**: Here is the screenshot of Tier 1 benchmarks of few Equity & Hybrid categories suggested by AMFI –

Category	Fund Category	Tier 1 Benchmark - NSE	S&P BSE Index	Crisil Indices
Equity	Multi Cap Fund	Nifty 500 Multicap 50:25:25	S&P BSE 500 TRI	
Equity	Large Cap Fund	NIFTY 100	S&P BSE 100 TRI	
Equity	Large & Mid Cap Fund	NIFTY Large Midcap 250	S&P BSE 250 Large MidCap TRI	
Equity	Mid Cap Fund	NIFTY Midcap 150	S&P BSE Midcap 150 TRI	
Equity	Small Cap Fund	NIFTY Smallcap 250	S&P BSE 250 SmallCap TRI	
Equity	ELSS	NIFTY 500	S&P BSE 500 TRI	
Equity	Flexi Cap Fund	NIFTY 500	S&P BSE 500 TRI	
Equity	Dividend Yield Fund	Nifty 500	S&P BSE 500	
Equity	Value Fund/Contra Fund	Nifty 500	S&P BSE 500	
Equity	Focused Fund	NIFTY 500	S&P BSE 500 TRI	
Hybrid	Conservative Hybrid Fund	NIFTY 50 Hybrid Composite Debt 15:85 Index		CRISIL Hybrid 85+15 Conservative Index
Hybrid	Balanced Hybrid Fund	NIFTY 50 Hybrid Composite debt 50:50 Index		CRISIL Hybrid 50+50 Moderate Index
Hybrid	Aggressive Hybrid Fund	NIFTY 50 Hybrid Composite Debt 65:35 Index		CRISIL Hybrid 35+65 Aggressive Index
Hybrid	Dynamic Asset Allocation / Balanced Advantage Fund	NIFTY 50 Hybrid Composite debt 50:50 Index		CRISIL Hybrid 50+50 - Moderate Index
Hybrid	Multi Asset Allocation Fund	NA		NA
Hybrid	Arbitrage Fund	NIFTY 50 Arbitrage		CRISIL Arbitrage Index
Hybrid	Equity Savings Fund	NIFTY Equity Savings		CRISIL Equity Savings Index

You can check the entire list of Tier 1 benchmarks on AMFI website at this link - https://www.amfiindia.com/research-information/other-data/listofbenchmarkindices

Benchmarks are useful for two purposes:

1. First, benchmark helps giving the reference point for comparing fund's returns. By comparing with benchmark, you will know your scheme is performing well or not. If it is consistently performing below benchmark, then it is definitely time to switch out.

2. Secondly, benchmark (esp. Tier 2 Benchmark) also gives you a fair idea of the type of portfolio Fund's scheme and the strategy fund is following. For example, Axis Focused 25 Fund is a Focused Category Fund and hence has Nifty 500 TRI as Tier 1 Benchmark but has taken Nifty 50 TRI as Tier 2 benchmark which shows that fund is more focused on Large Cap category.

111. WHAT IS TRI INDEX? DIFFERENCE BETWEEN TRI & PRI BENCHMARK

SEBI asked mutual fund houses to change the manner in which they were benchmarking the fund performance (As per Circular 'Benchmarking of Scheme's performance to Total Return Index' dated Jan 04, 2018). They were instructed to consider Total Return Index (TRI) as the new benchmark and everyone has already complied. Earlier they were using Price Return Index (PRI).

An investment vehicle like shares generates returns by two means i.e. capital appreciation and dividend payouts. Capital appreciation relates to the increase or decrease in the market price of the share. While measuring returns which a share actually generated, both of the above components play crucial role.

However, until recently, only one of them was considered for gauging performance. The Price Return Index (PRI) captured only the capital appreciation aspect of index constituents. It ignored the dividend payment component of the constituent shares. Example, if suppose SBI Bluechip Fund has a benchmark of BSE 100, then returns of BSE 100 index are calculated only through the capital appreciation of its constituent companies. Whatever dividends those companies paid was completely ignored. However, this dividend component is obviously not ignored in calculating SBI Bluechip fund's performance.

Typically, the dividend in an index is around 1.5 per cent annually. Since the previous indices are exclusive of the dividends, it understates the returns of the indices by about 1.5 per cent annually. To make things transparent and credible, Total Return Index (TRI) has been introduced. This index includes both the capital gains and dividend component to determine returns.

So BSE 100's TRI index will be called as BSE 200 TRI and so now, SBI Bluechip fund is benchmarked against this BSE 100 TRI.

For an identical basket of securities, the return of a total return index will always be greater than that of the price return index. It will be due to the additional payouts by way of dividends. With TRI coming in, the returns of the index will go up by 1-1.5 per cent yearly by default. Let us say that there was a particular scheme which claimed to beat the benchmark by 2.5 per cent in a year (before 2018). That outperformance has now come down to one per cent.

112. WHAT IS MUTUAL FUND CUT OFF TIMING?

As we know, NAV of the mutual fund changes daily, therefore the applicable NAV for any transaction depends primarily on the time at which the transaction request is received at the official points of acceptance. The Net Asset Value (NAV) at which you can purchase or sell units of your mutual fund scheme is determined by the cut-off time. Simply, the time you submit your application and money to the fund house determines the NAV allotment. In the mutual fund world, this is known as cut-off time. The cut-off time is different for liquid funds and debt & equity funds.

Liquid Funds (not for Ultra Short duration or other funds):

Application received of investment or redemption before 2 PM: Units are allotted on previous day's NAV.

Application received of investment or redemption after 2 PM: Units are allotted on same day's NAV

Debt & Equity Funds:

Application received of investment or redemption before 3 PM: Units are allotted at same day's NAV

Application received of investment or redemption after 3 PM: Units are allotted at next day's NAV

Many online portals and mutual fund accounts have a different cut-off time which is generally 2 PM for their investors. This is to help them process applications at the back end, and then route it to the fund house.

Our Take:

It's good to know cut-off timings, but there is no need to think too much about deadlines. It may matter if the investment or redemption amount is high otherwise, a day here or there won't make much difference in the long run.

113. HOW MUCH TIME WILL IT TAKE TO RECEIVE REDEMPTION PROCEEDS?

If you redeem your investment before cut-off time, you will get same day's NAV and money will get credited to your registered bank account after 1 working day (Transaction day+1) for Liquid and Debt funds and after maximum 2 days (Transaction day+2) for Equity Funds. Here are the details as on 1st Feb 2023:

Fund categories	Cut off time (PM)	Redemption payment cycle*
Debt	03:00	Trade day plus 1 day (T+1)
Equity	03:00	Trade day plus 2 days (T+2)
Hybrid	03:00	Trade day plus 2 days (T+2)
FoF Overseas	03:00	Trade day plus 5 days (T+5)**

*Including switch-in from other schemes
**In some cases, the redemption payment cycle for international funds is T+6 days

114. WHAT IS CONSOLIDATED ACCOUNT STATEMENT (CAS)?

Consolidated Account Statement (CAS) is a single account statement that consolidates financial transactions in all your mutual fund portfolios (consolidated by PAN number).

A CAS will be sent to you either on or before the tenth day of the succeeding month (For example 10th Feb), detailing all the transactions (buy, sell, switch) and holdings at the end of the month (Jan), including transaction charges paid to the distributor, across all schemes of all mutual funds. If you have a registered email address, this statement would be sent electronically. If not, it could be delivered to the physical address. You can also download these statements from CAMS & Karvy websites. Website Links:

CAMS: https://www.camsonline.com/Investors/Statements/Consolidated-Account-Statement

Karvy: https://mfs.kfintech.com/investor/General/Consolidated AccountStatement

This statement is very useful to have one view of your entire portfolio. You will continue to get separate statements sent by Fund house or Demat account etc.

Example of a CAS Statement –

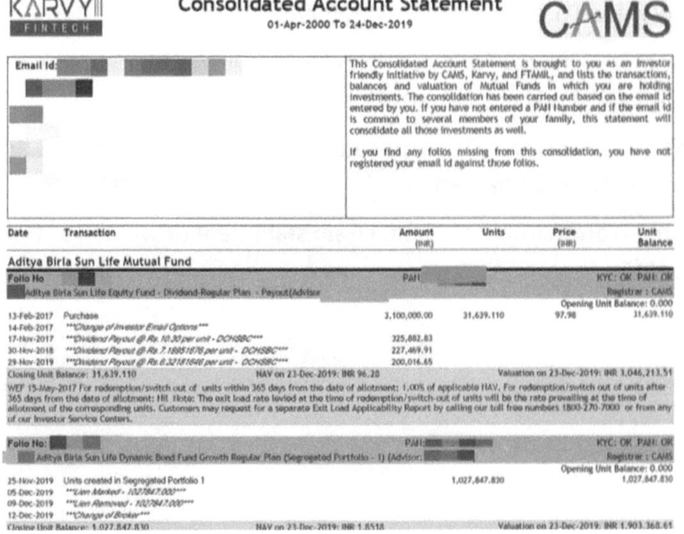

Consolidated Account Statement

01-Apr-2000 To 24-Dec-2019

This Consolidated Account Statement is brought to you as an investor friendly initiative by CAMS, Karvy, and FTAMIL, and lists the transactions, balances and valuation of Mutual Funds in which you are holding investments. The consolidation has been carried out based on the email id entered by you. If you have not entered a PAN Number and if the email id is common to several members of your family, this statement will consolidate all those investments as well.

If you find any folios missing from this consolidation, you have not registered your email id against those folios.

Date	Transaction	Amount (INR)	Units	Price (INR)	Unit Balance

Aditya Birla Sun Life Mutual Fund

Folio No   PAN   KYC: OK PAN: OK

Aditya Birla Sun Life Equity Fund - Dividend-Regular Plan - Payout(Advisor   Registrar : CAMS

Opening Unit Balance: 0.000

Date	Transaction	Amount (INR)	Units	Price (INR)	Unit Balance
13-Feb-2017	Purchase	3,100,000.00	31,639.110	97.98	31,639.110
14-Feb-2017	***Change of Investor Email Options***				
17-Nov-2017	***Dividend Payout @ Rs. 10.30 per unit - DCHSBC***	325,882.83			
30-Nov-2018	***Dividend Payout @ Rs 7.18951876 per unit - DCHSBC***	227,469.91			
29-Nov-2019	***Dividend Payout @ Rs 6.32181646 per unit - DCHSBC***	200,016.65			

Closing Unit Balance: 31,639.110   NAV on 23-Dec-2019: INR 96.28   Valuation on 23-Dec-2019: INR 3,046,213.51

WEF 15-May-2017 For redemption/switch out of units within 365 days from the date of allotment: 1.00% of applicable NAV. For redemption/switch out of units after 365 days from the date of allotment: Nil Note: The exit load rate levied at the time of redemption/switch-out of units will be the rate prevailing at the time of allotment of the corresponding units. Customers may request for a separate Exit Load Applicability Report by calling our toll free numbers 1800-270-7000 or from any of our Investor Service Centers.

Folio No: PAN: KYC: OK PAN: OK

Aditya Birla Sun Life Dynamic Bond Fund Growth Regular Plan (Segregated Portfolio - 1) (Advisor: Registrar : CAMS

Opening Unit Balance: 0.000

Date	Transaction	Amount (INR)	Units	Price (INR)	Unit Balance
25-Nov-2019	Units created in Segregated Portfolio 1		1,027,847.830		1,027,847.830
05-Dec-2019	***Lien Marked - 1027847.000***				
09-Dec-2019	***Lien Removed - 1027847.000***				
12-Dec-2019	***Change of Broker***				

Closing Unit Balance: 1,027,847.830   NAV on 23-Dec-2019: INR 1.8518   Valuation on 23-Dec-2019: INR 1,903,368.61

115. WHAT IS CAPITAL GAIN STATEMENT & HOW TO GET IT?

Capital gains refer to the income earned from the sale of bonds, mutual funds, or stocks by an individual. This type of income is subject to taxation under the provisions of the Income Tax Act. It is important for individuals to be aware of their total capital gains for a fiscal year in order to properly assess their tax liability and file accurate income tax returns. The details of these capital gains are available in your Capital Gain Statement. These statements also calculate your tax liability of Financial Year and can also calculate Indexation benefits on capital gain. If you are a Mutual Fund investor, you will need to give these statements to your Tax Consultant during ITR filing process to calculate the right Tax liability.

How to Download it?

Best way to download Capital Gain statement is through CAMS or Karvy website (RTAs of Mutual Funds). Both websites will give you consolidated capital gain statement of Mutual Funds serviced by them (Check the list in Q104). Here are links to download the capital gain statement –

CAMS: https://www.camsonline.com/Investors/Statements/Capital-Gain&Capital-Loss-statement

Karvy: https://mfs.kfintech.com/investor/General/CapitalGains LossAccountStatement

Here is an example of Capital Gain statement downloaded from CAMS:

Capital Gain / Loss Statement
For the period 01-Apr-2021 To 31-Mar-2022

CAMS

Email: [redacted]

[redacted]
[redacted]
[redacted]
Delhi
India
[redacted]

This statement provides your Investment Performance, Capital Gains and Income for the current and last Financial Years, consolidated across CAMS serviced funds. Statement will contain actual withdrawals made by you from your fund account, realised gains/losses on a FIFO basis and segregated as long term and short term. The statement now includes LTCG applicable for equity oriented schemes introduced in the Budget 2018. The statements will be provided for the previous and current financial year.

The consolidation has been carried out based on email id entered by you. If you do not have entered a PAN and if the email id is common to several members of your family, this statement will consolidate all those investments as well.

Should you find any folio missing in this consolidation, please check for the registration of your email id in the respective folio.

Capital Gain / Loss – Overall Summary

Summary of Capital Gains	01/04 to 15/06	16/06 to 15/09	16/09 to 15/12	16/12 to 15/03	16/03 to 31/03	Total
Short Term Capital Gain						
Full Value of Consideration (Total sale value)	0.00	0.00	0.00	150,000.00	0.00	150,000.00
Cost of acquisition (Purchase cost of redeemed units)	0.00	0.00	0.00	143,682.39	0.00	143,682.39
Capital Gains / Loss	0.00	0.00	0.00	6,317.83	0.00	6,317.83
Long Term Capital Gain with indexation						
Fair Market Value of capital asset as per section 55(2)(ac)	0.00	0.00	0.00	0.00	0.00	0.00
Full Value of Consideration (Total sale value)	0.00	0.00	0.00	0.00	0.00	0.00
Cost of acquisition (Purchase cost of redeemed units)	0.00	0.00	0.00	0.00	0.00	0.00
Capital Gains / Loss	0.00	0.00	0.00	0.00	0.00	0.00
Long Term Capital Gain without indexation						
Fair Market Value of capital asset as per section 55(2)(ac)	0.00	0.00	0.00	0.00	0.00	0.00
Full Value of Consideration (Total sale value)	0.00	0.00	0.00	0.00	0.00	0.00
Cost of acquisition (Purchase cost of redeemed units)	0.00	0.00	0.00	0.00	0.00	0.00
Capital Gains / Loss	0.00	0.00	0.00	0.00	0.00	0.00

* Refer Disclaimer at the end of Statement

Page 1 of 4

116. ROLE & IMPORTANCE OF INVESTMENT ADVISOR

Investment/ Financial Advisor is your financial doctor. They are the professionals with right qualifications and experience to manage your money and solving your queries. Following are the things you should expect from your investment advisors:

* <u>Understand your financial needs</u>: Advisor should have the holistic picture of you & your family's personal finance so that they can formulate your investment goals and objectives.

* <u>Help you develop realistic expectations</u>: He/she should set realistic expectations on your investments by discussing risk and reward profile of each asset and investment. Advisor should help you develop a strategy most comfortable for you.

* <u>Reduce your emotional quotient</u>: One of the big roles of advisor is to put space between you and your investments so that you don't make emotional decisions and you remain disciplined in your investments.

* __Do research & answer your questions__: Advisor should do detailed research on asset allocation or type of funds suited to you based on your risk profile, objectives and comfort. He/she should be able to solve all your queries.

* __Continually monitor your portfolio__: One of the most important roles of an advisor is to continually review your portfolio and make sure it is on track to achieve the goals. Also expect your advisor to work with you to adjust your portfolio in response to any significant change in market conditions, fund's objectives, your lifestyle, priorities, assets or responsibilities.

117. HOW TO CHOOSE A GOOD MF ADVISOR?

Choosing a good investment advisor is very like choosing a good doctor for your health. It can be tricky but a right choice can save huge money. Following should be your criteria to choose the right financial advisor:

1. __Reference__: Reference is the biggest parameter before you choose your doctor and same holds true for your financial advisor. You should talk to your friends and family and get the reference for the right person. You can also ask for references of their clients from the advisors too, to cross check their claims.

2. __Qualification__: You should check if your financial advisor is registered with AMFI or SEBI. You should additionally check their relevant graduation/post-graduation degrees.

3. __Experience__: Like doctors, experience of the financial advisor is very important criterion to choose. How many clients served? Years in the mutual fund industry?

4. __Infrastructure and Value added services__: Your advisor should have good infrastructure for ease of investment

process, portfolio tracking and reviews. A good MF advisor is not the one who can just advise you on MFs but should be able to help you in buying right life insurance and health covers, should be able to help you plan your estate. Your advisor should have a good team that covers each aspect of financial planning. The team should include a CA who can help with income tax filing and answering all tax related queries, lawyer for filing of the will.

5. <u>Individual over a company</u>: We would recommend you invest with an individual advisor rather than an advisory company as it will help you have a uniform face for long term. With the company, if the employee leaves, you have to deal with different advisors who may not be as per your expectations.

6. <u>Post your questions</u>: Before selecting an advisor, you should have a checklist of few questions to be asked to the advisor and choose him/her if they are answered satisfactorily. Many questions in this book could be a part of the checklist.

7. Once, you select an advisor watch out that he does not push you to invest in mutual funds of a certain fund house always, which may offer him a higher commission. He should not promise you unrealistic returns.

Mutual Fund Complaint Redressal

In 2011, SEBI launched a centralized online complaints redress system called "SCORES". The clear purpose of SCORES is to provide a platform to investors, whose complaints remain unresolved by the concerned listed Asset Management Companies or registered intermediaries even after approaching them directly. Intermediaries, here are those financial institutions that facilitate the distribution of funds between investors and issuers, such as banks, RTI agents and distributors who are registered with the SEBI. SCORES also provide a platform, overseen by SEBI, where investors can lodge, follow up and track a complaint. It is however advisable to directly approach the concerned entities in case of any complaints, before launching a complaint on SCORES. All these entities are required to have designated officials for handling issues relating to compliance and redressal of investor complaints.

Mutual Fund Toolkit

1. Always understand your risk profile before investing in Mutual Funds.

2. Before investing in Mutual Funds, first finalize the category you want to invest in.

3. Returns cannot be the only criterion for Mutual Fund selection. You should check the risk side too.

4. Mutual Funds are not stocks, do not keep changing them often.

5. First-time investor? You can start investing with ELSS (for Tax Saving) Funds or Index Funds (if Tax saving is not needed)

6. Hybrid Category is good for medium-term goals (3-5 years) or for investors who have retired.

7. Always check the trade volume of ETFs before investing

8. Always check the iNAV of the ETF before investing

9. Never invest in NFOs

10. Avoid investing in Dividend (IDCW) Plans

11. Avoid investing in high-risk Debt Funds. If you want to take more risk, hybrid or Equity categories are better.

12. Avoid investing in Solution-Oriented Plans

13. Avoid investing in more than 5 Equity Funds and 3 Debt Funds.

14. Invest in Sector funds only if you understand the cycles of that sector otherwise avoid.

15. Calendar and Rolling Returns are better measures to evaluate fund's performance than Trailing returns

16. There is NO best day to do SIP. The best day to do SIP is the next day of Your Salary

17. Normal, Simple Monthly SIPs are the best way to invest in Equity Mutual Funds. Avoid other complications.

18. Invest in Direct plans if you can manage your investments and fund reviews yourself or have an advisor or portfolio manager for the same. (like a subscription to InvestYadnya's Model Portfolios)

19. Invest in Regular Plans if you do not want to manage all paperwork/operational work associated with investing or do not have time for Mutual Fund reviews or you want to have all your investment in one window like in one Demat account or you an NRI and have very limited option to invest in Direct Plans.

20. Always check the Expense ratio of the fund before investing. Also, keep tracking that number while you are invested.

21. Avoid investing very large lump sum (w.r.t. networth) in Equity Funds

22. Never sell mutual funds in panic. Sell funds when your goal is complete or near completion or when performance is consistently bad and not in panic.

Acroynms

AIF	Alternate Investment Fund
AMC	Asset Management Company
AMFI	Association of Mutual funds of India
AUM	Asset Under Management
CAGR	Compound Annual Growth Rate
CAS	Consolidated Account Statement
CBLO	Collateralized Borrowing and Lending Obligation
CII	Cost Inflation Index
CMB	Cash Management Bills
DDT	Dividend Distribution Tax
ELSS	Equity Linked Saving Scheme
ETF	Exchange-Traded Fund
FATCA	Foreign Account Tax Compliance Act
FMP	Fixed Maturity Plans
FOF	Funds of Funds
IFA	Independent Financial Advisor
IPO	Initial Public Offer
KYC	Know Your Customer
LTCG	Long Term Capital Gain
MD	Modified Duration
MFU	Mutual Fund Utility
MIP	Monthly Income Plan
MIS	Monthly Income Scheme

NAV	Net Asset Value
NBFC	Non-Banking Financial Company
NCD	Non-
NFO	New Fund Offer
NPS	National Pension System
NSC	National Saving Certificate
PRI	Price Return Index
REIT	Real Estate Investment Trust
RIA	Registered Investment Advisor
SDL	State Development Loans
SGB	Sovereign Gold Bonds
SIP	Systematic Investment Plan
SLR	Statutory Liquidity Ratio
STCG	Short Term Capital Gains
STP	Systematic Transfer Plan
SWP	Systematic Withdrawal Plan
T-Bills	Treasury Bills
TDS	Tax Deduction at Source
TER	Total Expense Ratio
TRI	Total Return Index
VIP	Value Averaging Investment Plan
XIRR	Extended Internal Rate of Return
YTM	Yield to Maturity

GLOSSARY

Alpha	Returns over and above the predicted ones.
Arbitrage	Simultaneous purchase of securities on one stock exchange and sale of the same security on another stock exchange at profitable pricing.
Benchmark	Anything against which you can compare your results The Sensex and Nifty is commonly used as benchmarks. However, depending on the fund in question, there are a plethora of them.
Blue Chip Stocks	Stocks of well-established and financially solid enterprises with a long history of dividend payments and other excellent investment characteristics
Brokerage	The commissions you pay your broker for allowing you to buy and sell securities.
Capital Appreciation	A rise in the price or value of an asset.
Closed-Ended Fund	A type of mutual fund which issues a fixed number of units while raising the capital in NFO and these units are traded on the stock exchange. No new units are created and new investments are accepted.

Compounding	The appreciation in the value of an investment as a result of the interest generated on the principal as well as cumulative interest
Credit Rating	Independent rating organisations rate all debt issued by firms or governments based on their ability to repay. AAA-rated debt, for example, is good, but BB-rated debt is not.
Default	Failure to pay the debt which includes interest and principal. It happens when the borrower does not timely makes the payment, misses the payments, avoids or stops payments.
Derivatives	A contract between two or more parties whose value is dependent on the underlying financial security or set of securities.
Diversification	Purchasing shares in a variety of companies operating in several industries to reduce investment risk.
Dividend	On their investment, shareholders receive a part of the company's earnings. It's commonly expressed as a percentage of the stock's current value.
Dividend Yield	Divide the total dividends paid over the previous 12 months by the most recent share price.
Exchange-Traded Fund (ETF)	ETFs are similar to mutual funds, but they are traded on the stock exchange and can be bought and sold like stocks.

Exit Load	These are the charges which are liable to be paid in a case an investor exits a fund before a specified time frame.
Expense Ratio	To manage the money, a mutual fund house/AMC incurs some expenses such as fund management fees, agent commissions, registrar fees, auditor fees, advertising expenses, etc. To manage these expenses, fund houses charge a fee for their services which is called the Expense Ratio.
Floating Rate	It's an interest rate that fluctuates with the rest of the market or according to an index.
Fundamental Analysis	It is the process of determining the stocks real or fair market value by analysing the economics and financials of the underlying business.
Gilt Funds	Gilt funds are mutual funds that only invest in government securities.
Grandfathered	Waived off (No tax payable)
Hedge	A risk-reducing transaction on an existing investment position.
Hedge Fund	A fund that can use a variety of strategies to boost returns.
Index	Based on the performance of the stock, a statistical measure of the state of the stock market. The Sensex and Nifty are two examples.

Index Fund	A mutual fund that invests in securities that match or represent a specified index. BSE 30 index, for example, is a fund that aims to replicate BSE Sensex's returns.
Indexation	Indexation means adjustment of gains with respect to Inflation i.e. subtracting the impact of inflation on your returns and then paying taxes.
KYC	Know Your Customer is a mandatory requirement by SEBI for declaring identity and address proof for the purpose of investing.
Liquidity	This relates to how simple it is to buy and sell securities on the market. It also refers to how simple it is for investors to turn their securities into cash.
Lock-in Period	This is the amount of time that the investment can't be withdrawn once it's been made.
Market Capitalization	It is the total value of the issued shares of a publicly-traded company; it is arrived at by multiplying all the outstanding shares with the current market price.
Net Asset Value	On a given date or time, it is the value per share of a mutual fund.
Open-Ended Fund	A mutual fund that does not have any limit for issuing units. The units of the fund can be issued and redeemed anytime.
P/E Ratio	The ratio values the company by measuring its current price relative to its earnings. It ratio is calculated by diving the share price with the earnings per share.

Passive Management	It is a style of fund management that tracks a particular index and has no active involvement of the fund manager.
Portfolio	For an individual, A portfolio is a person's collection of financial investments. For a Mutual Fund, the existing holdings of the fund in various financial securities are referred to as a portfolio.
Redemption	The act of taking money out of a mutual fund that has been invested.
Repatriable	Ability to move the liquid financial assets from a foreign country to the country of origin of the investor.
Rupee Cost Averaging	Regularly investing a set amount in specific security over a period of time. When the price is low, the investor buys more shares, and when the price is high, the investor buys a lesser number of shares.
Section 80C	A section under Income Tax Act, 1961 that states the exemptions for income tax.
Side-Pocketing	Side pocketing is a process where riskier or illiquid investments are segregated from the actual portfolio. Once side-pocketing has been done, only the present unitholders are entitled to its share. New investors won't receive the proceeds from the securities which are side-pocketed.
Volatile	Volatility represents the swings of assets values from their historic mean. It is a statistical measure of the dispersion of returns. Volatility can be measured as Beta, Standard Deviation, etc.

Yield to Maturity (YTM)	The rate of return an investor will receive if he or she holds a bond until it matures.
Zero-Coupon Securities	It is a bond that does not pay interest. It is issued at a discount to face value and at the maturity, the face value is paid back. The difference between the issue price and face value is the profit for the investor.

Credits

News website:

- * Economictimes.indiatimes.com
- * www.financialexpress.com
- * www.businesstoday.in
- * www.thehindubusinessline.com
- * www.business-standard.com
- * www.livemint.com
- * timesofindia.indiatimes.com

Financial Portals

- * Fund-o-meter by InvestYadnya.in
- * Valueresearchonline.com
- * Moneycontrol.com
- * www.bankbazaar.com
- * www.morningstar.in
- * www.amfiindia.com
- * www.investopedia.com
- * investor.sebi.gov.in
- * www.karvy.com
- * www.paisabazaar.com

Mutual Fund Companies Websites

- * www.icicipruamc.com
- * www.hdfcfund.com

* www.idfcmf.com
* www.franklintempletonindia.com
* www.sbimf.com
* assetmanagement.kotak.com
* www.axismf.com
* www.utimf.com
* www.hdfcmfinvestwise.com
* www.reliancemutual.com
* mutualfund.birlasunlife.com

Blogs

* www.arthayantra.com/blogs/
* www.fundsindia.com/blog
* www.jagoinvestor.com
* www.advisorkhoj.com
* www.quora.com
* www.relakhs.com/MutualFunds
* www.personalfn.com
* cafemutual.com
* www.charteredclub.com
* www.basunivesh.com
* scripbox.com/blog
* www.getmoneyrich.com
* youtube.com/InvestYadnya